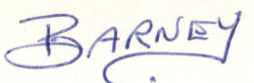

Food Service Purchasing:
Principles and Practices

Food Service Purchasing:
Principles and Practices

Hugh J. Kelly

Lebhar-Friedman Books
Chain Store Publishing Corp.
A Subsidiary of Lebhar-Friedman, Inc.
New York

Second printing, 1978.

Copyright © 1976, Chain Store Publishing Corporation
425 Park Avenue, New York, N.Y. 10022

All rights reserved. No part of this book is to be reproduced in any form or by any means without permission in writing from the publisher.

Printed in the United States of America
Library of Congress Catalog Card Number: 76–49750
International Standard Book Number: 0–912016–55–8

*To my wife, Donna McAuley,
for her love, wisdom, and commitment.*

Contents

Preface		ix
Chapter 1	Purchasing and Your Profits	1
Chapter 2	Organizing Your Purchasing Function	9
Chapter 3	Source Selection	23
Chapter 4	Price Considerations	33
Chapter 5	Buying Strategy	61
Chapter 6	Food Buying	81
Chapter 7	Portion Control and Frozen Prepared Food Items	101
Chapter 8	The Purchase of Alcoholic Beverages	109
Chapter 9	The Purchase of Tabletop Items and Operating Supplies	119
Chapter 10	Equipment Programs in the Food Service Industry	129
Chapter 11	The Purchase of Capital Items	137
Chapter 12	Purchasing Procedures and Controls	147
Chapter 13	Training Purchasing Personnel	161
Chapter 14	Purchasing and Quality Control	169
Chapter 15	Service and Vendor Relations	177
Chapter 16	Value Analysis As a Purchasing Tool	183
Chapter 17	Communications	191
Chapter 18	Centralized Versus Decentralized Purchasing	201

Chapter 19	The Sales Side of the Buyer's Life	207
Chapter 20	Services Available to the Food Service Industry	213
Chapter 21	The Concept of Materials Management	221
Appendix		229
Index		233

Preface

In the early years of my purchasing career at General Foods Corp., I frequently complained about the lack of material written on the subject of purchasing in the food industry. It seemed to me that every purchasing text or magazine I encountered talked about purchasing for the steel industry, the machine tool industry, electric utilities, and appliance and auto companies. Despite my interest in learning more about the purchasing profession, I simply could not find adequate written material that related specifically to the procurement problems of the food industry.

Having made a transition to a more tightly defined segment of the food industry—the food service industry—I found that the lack of written material on the specific purchasing problems of this highly complex, very specialized industry sub-group was even more apparent.

During the late 1960's and early 1970's, I had occasion to participate in a number of food service industry seminars in various parts of the United States. I was struck by the frequency with which these gatherings addressed themselves to procurement problems, and by the growing interest in, and concern for, this area. This was particularly obvious in food service industry operations executives, who, while not responsible for the day-to-day procurement activities of their companies, realized the direct impact that purchasing performance had on their profits. What I had lamented ten years earlier at General

Foods was an even bigger problem in the food service industry. Purchasing had come of age!

Hence, when I had the opportunity to prepare a text on this subject, I was delighted to take on the project—the day when purchasing was considered a semiclerical function had passed into history. Today, I am happy to report, that situation has been reversed, and the purchasing function is regarded as a key source of corporate profitability.

I hope that you will approach this book in the same context as I wrote it—as a practical operating tool to be used by the person in the food service industry who wishes to derive maximum return from the operation of his purchasing function.

In order to make this text more useful to the individual reader, and to the food service student, I have included a list of questions relating to the material in each chapter. These questions have been designed to help you test your comprehension of the material covered in each chapter, and to provide a basis for you to develop your ideas and recommendations from the chapter.

It is my hope that in answering the questions, you will not restrict yourself to the material contained in the chapter, but rather that you will use that material as a jumping-off point to formulate your own ideas as to how each question should be answered. This approach should be particularly beneficial to those who are already engaged in the food service industry and who can consequently utilize their own work experience to answer the question. It is my hope that you will make every effort to answer the questions at the end of each chapter, since they are designed to give you maximum return for the time you expend with this volume.

What follows represents the synthesis of both first-hand experience and fundamental learning that I have accumulated during my eighteen years of procurement experience with two of the real giants of the American food industry. Were it not for the innovative attitudes I encountered at both General Foods and Howard Johnson's, this book would never have seen the light of day.

Although I have always had very definite ideas about how a food service procurement operation should function, a text of this scope could obviously not be written without the help and input of many other people. If I were to list individually all those who had contributed to compiling this book, it would include a virtual directory of the many fine purchasing people and vendor personnel I have worked with over the past eighteen years. Many of my ideas and concepts were triggered by comments from these individuals. To all of them I owe a debt of thanks for their input to this work.

However, I would particularly like to acknowledge the help of my first purchasing mentor, Mr. Max Snyder of General Foods Corporation, and my associates in the purchasing department at the Howard Johnson Company, especially Mr. Bruce Dalrymple, Vice President of Purchasing. I would like to recognize my former secretary, Mrs. Shirley Hair, for her patience and commitment in helping me to assemble this book. Finally, I acknowledge the support and good sense of Ms. Julie Laitin, the senior editor of Chain Store Publishing Corp., who worked with me on this manuscript.

A special note of recognition must be given to Howard B. Johnson, Chairman of the Board and President of Howard Johnson's, for his willingness to allow me, as a newcomer to his organization in 1967, to structure a purchasing department along the lines which to me seemed most logical, based on previous experience, and to begin the development of a purchasing philosophy and tool chest of purchasing techniques now generally regarded to be among the finest in the food service industry. This willingness to try a new approach created an environment of creativity and innovation which encouraged the development of successful new systems. Without the assistance of these people, this book would not have reached your hands. To all, thanks.

It's unwise to pay too much,
but it's worse to pay too little.

When you pay too much, you
lose a little money . . . that is all.

When you pay too little, you
sometimes lose everything,
because the thing you bought
was incapable of doing the
thing it was bought to do.

The common law of business
balance prohibits paying a
little and getting a lot . . . it can't
be done. If you deal with the
lowest bidder, it is well to add
something for the risk you
run, and if you do that you will
have enough to pay for something better.

    John Ruskin   (1819–1900)

1

Purchasing and Your Profits

THE IMPORTANCE OF PURCHASING

When the restaurant operator or customer or industry analyst commonly thinks about ways of improving restaurant profitability, the first thing that comes to mind is increasing volume. This is normally done through a wide variety of promotions, advertising price specials, and the like. When it comes to improving profitability, however, most people consider improved margins in the labor and controllable expense categories, and in the cost of goods to be the key to improved profitability.

Only within the last few years have successful operators begun to recognize the importance of sound purchasing practices. In today's economy, the old philosophy, "I really don't care what an item costs as long as I can pass that cost on to my customer" is as old as a wood-burning cooking stove! Under the cost pressures that affect all types of businesses, operators simply can't afford to have such a relaxed and careless attitude about purchasing if they want to keep their businesses functioning.

Today the attitude must be, "How can I bring my costs to an absolute minimum while maintaining my standard quality?" Achieving this minimum cost level results in maximum efficiency and profitability of the operation. Ignoring it, or giving it only secondary importance, can result in the failure of an operation.

Statistics on retail busniess failures indicate that eating and drinking establishments account for approximately 20% of all such failures on a year-to-year basis. In the last few years the total amount of funds involved in restaurant failures has been running in excess of $100 million per year. If you were unaware of the vulnerability of the restaurant, these brief statistics should provide a rather grim warning. Restaurant failures are most likely to occur in the second year of operation, after the euphoria of the starting-up period and its attendant expenses have been replaced by the bitter realities of the profit and loss statement.

Lest anyone assume that large restaurant operators have an immunity to this disease, let me point out that almost every large chain has an occasional unit that "just couldn't make it," and that every so often an entire chain will collapse when its cost of operation consistently exceeds revenue from those operations. In the last few years there have been at least three major chains in New York City alone that have been unable to continue profitable operations. Thus, while the individual operator faces great business risks in opening an eating or drinking establishment, his cousin in the large food service corporation carries the same burden.

HOW PURCHASING INFLUENCES PROFITS

Before we probe the considerations of purchasing, let's look at how purchasing can influence restaurant profits. Very simply stated, any saving in purchase cost is directly reflected in an increased operating profit so long as other costs remain constant. Therefore, clearly, any reduction in the purchase cost of the necessary materials can be considered as dropping to the "bottom line."

For example, let's say that Restaurant A has become known for its prime ribs of beef. It features this item at a special promotion price of $4.95 for an eight-ounce portion. The normal cost to the operator for this eight-ounce portion with the accompanying vegetables and garnish is $1.50 per portion. If, however, as a result of astute market timing, good supplier selection, and competitive bidding, the operator is able to reduce the total cost per portion from $1.50 to $1.25 without sacrificing the quality of the meal, this extra

25¢ drops directly to the bottom, or profit, line on the operating statement and becomes additional profit for the operator. While admittedly over-simplified, this example represents the essence of what this book is all about: how anyone from the individual operator to the large chain can use purchasing practices to lower his costs and increase his profitability.

FIXED VS. CONTROLLABLE COSTS

It is a generally accepted fact that such items as labor, utilities, cleaning services, laundry, taxes, insurance, rodent and pest control, garbage removal, etc. will continue to increase despite efforts to keep them stable. Naturally, some of these costs can be decreased by reducing the quality of service in a particular area. For example, hiring seven waitresses instead of nine will decrease your expenses. However, if your operations and services remain fixed, you can assume that all related costs will continue to move inexorably upward on a year-to-year basis.

That leaves us with the cost of food and supplies as the only really controllable expenses in the restaurant operation. There are really two ways that this control is best exercised: first, by doing a better buying job, and second, by selective substitution of materials to improve the cost/sales/profit ratio. These are as important for the individual operator as they are for the large, national, multiunit chains, although there may be different considerations involved for each. For the individual operator it may mean trying to pick the best time and supplier for the purchase of a crate of eggs. For the chain, it may mean trying to arrange the best circumstances possible to fix a price commitment on a million pounds of beef or seafood. In either case, the quality (price/value relationship) of the purchase will have a large part in determining the profitability of that operation during the period in which the merchandise is consumed.

The price/value relationship is that combination of factors in each purchase decision which warrants the purchase. It takes into account the relative importance of the cost of the merchandise and its utilitarian worth. A good word to summarize this relationship is *quality*. This does not mean simply the grade of a food item (Grade A or Grade B), but rather the degree to which the price of the item corresponds to its value in meeting its specific intended purpose.

Unlike the costs of labor, utilities, taxes, etc., the cost of food products fluctuates widely (wildly at times, as in the case with sugar and vegetable oils) and cyclically, as with beef, pork, poultry, and seafood. While escalating food costs are a problem, at least there is enough variation in them so that the astute purchaser can take advantage of the most economical time to buy various items. This timing is a critical element in an effective buying program and will be developed in further detail later.

PURCHASING ACTIVITIES: HOW THEY CAN REDUCE EFFICIENCY

Ordering

There are many different types of purchasing activity which occur within the restaurant environment. If these activities are not carefully and regularly checked and controlled, they can reduce the efficiency and profitability of a restaurant operation considerably. The most frequent, and perhaps least professional, is the ordering of items. While this is really a simple clerical activity, it is the first step in purchasing. Even at this level, many restaurants fail to use proper controls. For example, when the operator needs a crate of lettuce or a case of ketchup, he merely calls the first purveyor who comes to mind and asks him to deliver it as soon as possible. All too often he does this without checking the price from that purveyor or comparing it with the prices from other purveyors. This can lead to considerable and unnecessary overexpenditures.

Partial Systematizing of Purchasing Activities

Another buying activity which can diminish profitability involves partial attempts to systematize the purchasing activity that end up falling short of maximum efficiency. In these situations, operators carefully interview potential suppliers and judiciously seek the most competitive bid. At the same time, however, they may neglect to order items in quantity, which also helps keep prices down. They may also request specialized delivery arrangements which the purveyor cannot provide without adding to the delivery charge. Or they may ignore the cyclical nature of many food prices and therefore purchase $\frac{1}{52}$ of their yearly requirement in each of the 52 weeks of that year. A far more effective method of purchasing is to group items to be purchased and place orders at times when the market price is lower.

An excellent example of this type of inefficiency is the operator who asks his produce vendor for daily deliveries, or, even worse, for weekend deliveries which require overtime wages. The vast majority of restaurants can adapt to a thrice weekly delivery of produce items on a Monday, Wednesday, Friday schedule. Similarly, the operator who fails to maximize the quantity which he can accept on each delivery is forcing his supplier to charge him the higher price which almost always accompanies the small volume order.

Procurement by the Chef

Procurement by the chef or cook is another problem that can reduce the efficiency of a restaurant. Experience has shown that a good chef must necessarily devote most of his time to the actual planning and preparation of the food. In most cases asking the chef to assume this responsibility in addition to his other duties places an unreasonable burden on him. Depending on the size of the operation, this job should be handled either by the owner, by the unit manager, or by specifically assigned individuals with purchasing training. Clearly, a man with a background in purchasing and with experience in repeated negotiation with vendors will consistently out-perform an individual whose specialty lies in another field and who has many other responsibilities in addition to purchasing.

Because the purchasing activity has a direct impact on profits, it deserves as much attention as any other profit-making segment of the business. The owner of a small restaurant would not dream of delegating his menu planning and pricing to a subordinate untrained in these areas. All too frequently, however, he will ask a person without formal training to assume the responsibility for purchasing.

Similarly, a surprising number of large chains lose efficiency through inconsistent guidelines. For example, they pay careful attention to centralizing such functions as marketing, personnel, public relations, architecture, design, and construction at the headquarters level. Yet they allow fairly broad local initiative with regard to purchasing. This means that their purchasing is decentralized and often poorly controlled. Senior executives of the company explain this apparent inconsistency by saying something like, "The purchasing function just doesn't lend itself to centralization," or even more upsetting, "Purchasing is essentially a clerical function, so we try to assign it at the lowest possible level." Attitudes like this were quite popular twenty years ago. Recently, however, with constantly rising prices for most things, the purchasing profession has assumed a newfound respect, as operators recognize its potential contributions to corporate profits. It is with this respect very much in mind that we will treat the many sides of the purchasing job in the coming chapters.

HOW DOES THE SIZE OF YOUR OPERATION AFFECT PURCHASING?

Throughout this book, there will be references to purchasing for both the small restaurant or restaurants owned by one person and the medium-or large-sized chain. In most cases the purchasing techniques are the same for both operations. In fact, the small operation is actually a microcosm of the larger one.

One significant difference between the two, however, is the difficulty of developing purchasing power (some prefer to call it "leverage" or "clout") when buying for the small operation. A buyer for the large operation who utilizes his purchasing power will consistently get better prices and value in his purchases (also referred to as the *price/value relationship*). While a buyer for a small chain may be every bit as astute in his purchasing activities, his lack of concentrated volume in procurement activities will give him less power to strike the same type of deal.

Another important difference between buying for the small and large restaurant operation is the amount of time required to put purchasing decisions into effect. In the large chain a buyer may require up to sixty days or more to present, purchase, and obtain an item on the menu. This may not necessarily be a sign of corporate immobility, but simply a result of such factors as the timing of menu cycles, the printing time required for the menus themselves, and the promotion plans for a large number of restaurants. As for the small operation, on the other hand, purchase decisions can usually be reached in a very few days.

As we treat specific areas of purchasing for the restaurant industry, we will attempt to pinpoint those categories where additional differences do exist. The key idea for the small operator to remember, however, is that in most cases, bigness is not a prerequisite for successful purchasing activity. While a small operator may not have the financial resources to go out and purchase a year's supply of shrimp because the price has dropped to a five-year low, he can still approach his supplier of shrimp and negotiate an extended contract at a fixed price when he feels the market is favorable. Many buyers are often surprised to see how cooperative a vendor will be if they take the time to request his assistance in taking advantage of an attractive price situation.

If you are a small buyer, never hesitate to ask your suppliers for legitimate price concessions. After all, the worst that can happen is that the vendor will decline to provide them. However, you will be pleasantly surprised quite often to see how willing your suppliers will be to cooperate with you in providing services which you may have felt would only be available to a giant chain.

Chapter 1 Questions

1. Explain how a reduction in food costs affects the "bottom line" of the food service profit and loss statement.

2. Discuss what is meant by the term "purchasing power" or "purchasing leverage."

3. In what ways can the buyer for the small restaurant operation emulate his counterpart in the major food service chain?

4. What is meant by the price/value relationship in discussing purchasing activity?

5. Explain the two most significant differences between purchasing for the individual restaurant and purchasing for the large chain.

2

Organizing Your Purchasing Function

ESTABLISH CLEAR GUIDELINES

As with any important responsibility, the purchasing function must be established along clearly defined lines. All company personnel connected with the purchasing function must clearly understand who has the purchasing responsibility, what that responsibility amounts to, and how it is executed. The people who have the direct responsibility for purchasing must understand the exact limits of their authority, what approval and authority are required for certain purchases, and the specific job duties they are expected to perform.

A logical place to start this type of structuring is at the beginning, with a basic organization chart and a preliminary job description for each person involved in the purchasing function. Sample organization charts for both the individual operation and the large chain are shown in Figures 1 and 2. Figures 3 and 4 give sample job descriptions for purchasing personnel in both the individual operation and the large chain. However, keep in mind that each individual restaurant has its own particular needs that may require a somewhat different approach to both the organization chart and the job description. Therefore, consider these figures as examples for illustrative purposes only, to be used as guidelines, not hard and fast rules, for the reader.

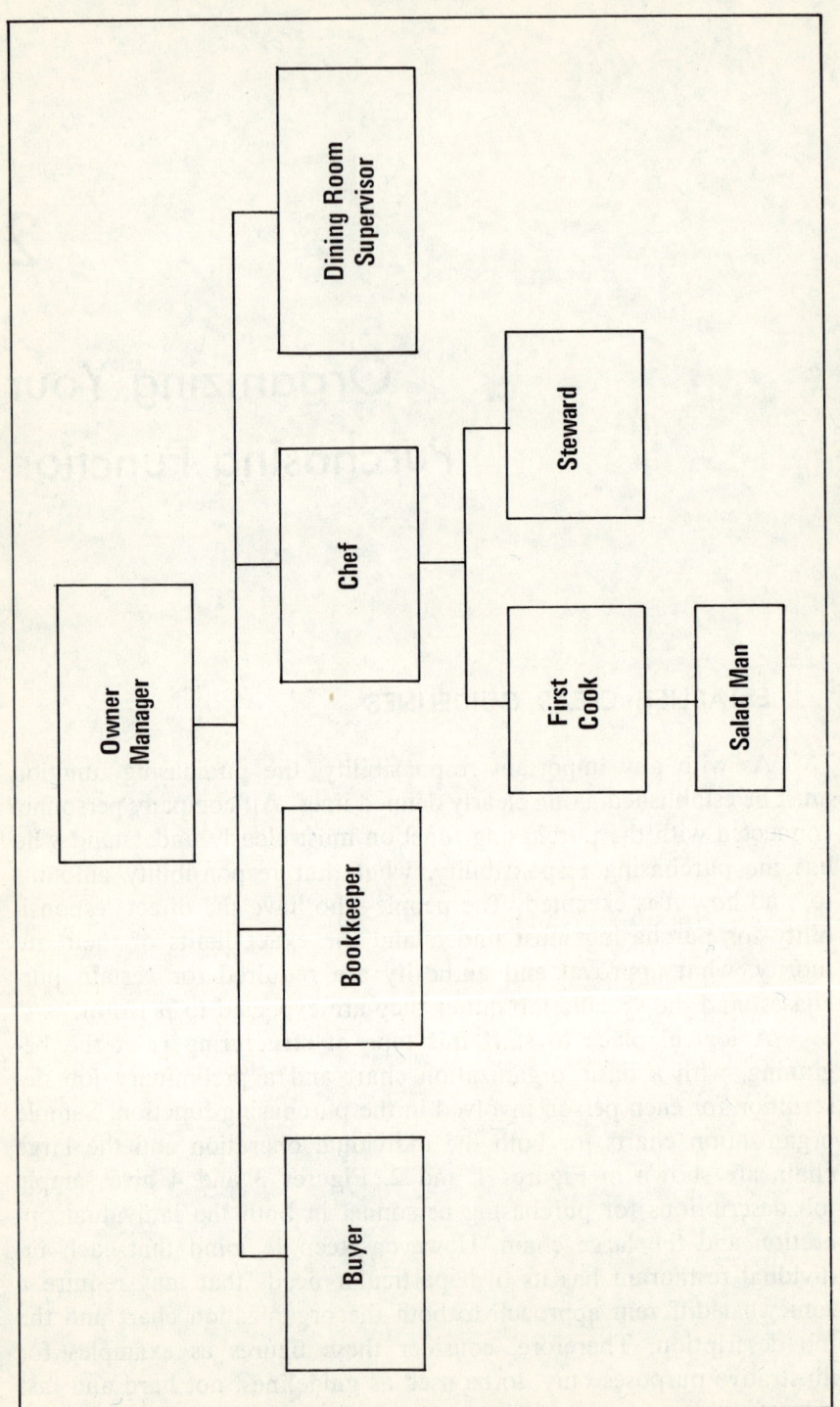

Figure 1 Organization chart for the individual unit

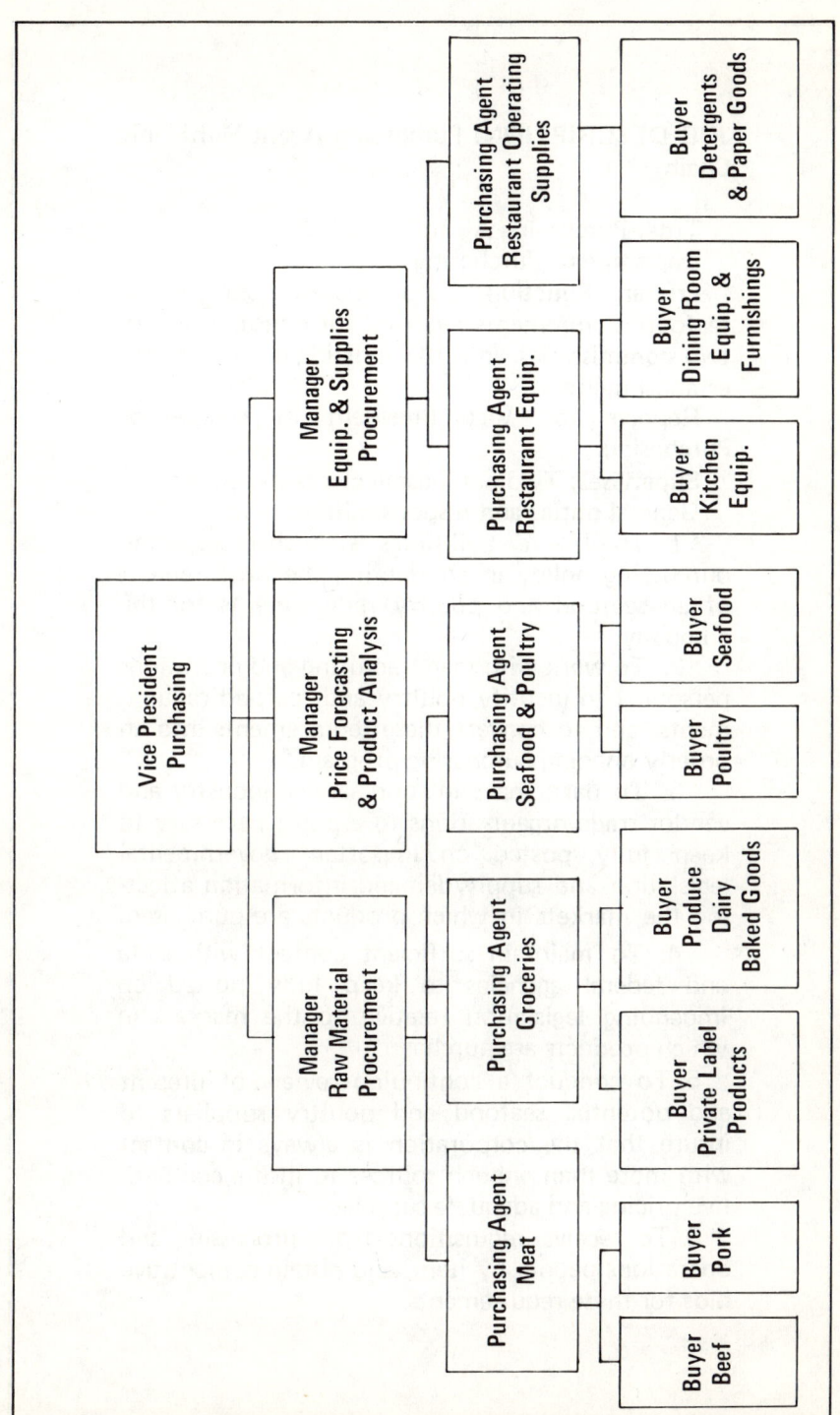

Figure 2 Organization chart for the multi-unit chain

JOB DESCRIPTION: Purchasing Agent-Multi-Unit Chain

Title: Purchasing Agent
Department: Purchasing
Primary Function: To purchase all poultry and seafood requirements required for consumption in two commissaries and 143 individual food service establishments.
Reports to: Vice President in charge of Purchasing.
Supervises: Two purchasing clerks/expediters
General duties and responsibilities:

1. To observe at all times established corporate purchasing policy in conducting the procurement of all seafood and poultry requirements for the company.

2. To work with manufacturing and operations personnel to identify poultry and seafood requirements, and to convert these requirements into an orderly ongoing purchasing program.

3. To participate in food service industry and vendor trade organizations to a point necessary to keep fully posted on important governmental legislation and supply/demand information affecting the markets in which products are purchased.

4. To maintain sufficient contact with state and federal agencies to keep fully posted on impending legislation relative to the markets in which products are purchased.

5. To conduct a continuing review of present and potential seafood and poultry suppliers to insure that the corporation is always in contact with more than enough sources to insure competitive pricing and adequate supplies.

6. To receive requisitions from processing and operations people by item, and obtain competitive bids for these requirements.

Figure 3 Job description for a purchasing agent in a multi-unit chain

7. To place orders with vendors on price, quality and delivery terms most favorable to the corporation.

8. To follow up on all shipments to insure that product is delivered on time and in the proper condition, and at the proper price.

9. To arrange outside storage for advanced purchase materials when necessary.

10. To negotiate long-term contracts with vendors when such action seems appropriate to minimize the company's cost of these raw materials.

11. To provide a quarterly forecast to top management showing price and supply trends for each of the poultry and seafood items being purchased for the company.

12. To constantly review the marketplace for new products which might enhance or replace seafood and poultry items presently being purchased.

JOB DESCRIPTION: Buyer

Primary function to purchase and expedite materials and equipment necessary to support the efficient and economical operation of the food service facility.

Reports to: Owner/manager
Supervises: Purchasing secretary/clerk
General duties and responsibilities:

1. Identifies material and equipment requirements through direct observation and communication with owner and chef.

2. Identifies potential sources of supply and conducts preliminary review of supplier capabilities.

3. Solicits quotations from vendors who have had previous experience supplying these products, or those new vendors who appear to be capable of supplying them.

4. Reviews requisitions received from kitchen and forwards them to selected vendors in the form of purchase orders.

5. Follows up vendors to insure delivery of merchandise on time, and in the proper condition.

6. Reviews receiving documents and quality control reports, and attaches them to supplier invoice as backup material before forwarding to the bookkeeper for payment.

7. Performs such other duties as directed by the owner/manager.

Figure 4   Job description for a buyer in an individual operation

BUYING AUTHORITY AND APPROVAL

Once the fundamental guidelines of organization chart and job description have been established, the next important area that should be clearly spelled out is the buying authority. In the case of the owner who does his own buying, the buying authority is his to handle as he chooses. A word of caution here: If you are an owner/buyer, you should recognize that purchasing can be a double-edged sword. If you are not careful and are overly zealous in your buying, you can make several mistakes. If you buy too large a quantity of a particular item at a fixed price, your operation can be hurt if the market price for that particular item drops. On the other hand, if you fail to recognize an upward price movement and therefore don't cover your requirement, your company will have to pay substantially higher prices for material which you should have bought earlier.

If you are an owner who chooses to delegate purchasing responsibility to an employee, your first step should be to spell out very clearly what buying authority is being delegated. If you want to allow an employee to sign for only those purchase orders below a maximum amount, you should inform him of this when you assign this responsibility to him. Regardless of how competent an employee is, placing a maximum value on purchase orders which the employee may sign for protects you and him. If the order exceeds that value, the employee should know that he cannot sign it without the owner's approval.

In the case of the individual operation this value might be established at $500.00. In the case of the chain operation a buyer may be given authority to enter into a purchase contract up to a maximum value of $20,000. On purchase decisions in excess of that amount, the buyer should be required to inform his immediate supervisor, who then has the authority to approve commitments of up to $50,000. This supervisor may then be required to approach a corporate officer for approval of all purchase decisions in excess of $50,000.

Without clearly defined buying authority assigned to each person handling the purchasing responsibility, and without established approval lines indicated before the purchase, there is always the unpleasant possibility of a buyer overstepping not only his authority but also his competency in making commitments which will be legally binding on his employer.

The recent collapse of a major U.S. bank on Long Island was

primarily attributed to an employee in the bank's foreign currency department speculating in foreign currencies. Speculation in foreign currencies is not too different from speculation in the commodity markets or speculation on the part of a buyer who purchases a large quantity of a particular product with the expectation that the price will rapidly increase and he will be able to sell his excess supply at a profit. All too often, however, he finds that the price declines instead, and he must sell his excess inventory at a loss.

ESTABLISH A LIMITED NUMBER OF QUALIFIED PURCHASERS

In addition to establishing guidelines for buying authority and approval, you should also be certain that the number of people involved in the purchasing activity is clearly identified. Most people want to perform as a buyer. Restaurant operations people, who would never dream of writing advertising copy or designing a new room in the building, will not hesitate to sit down with a supplier and negotiate a long term contract which could very well be contrary to the best interests of the company. Over the years psychologists have pondered man's desire to be a buyer; perhaps it comes from the fact that we have all bought food at some time in our lives, and we therefore consider ourselves experts in the field. In the restaurant industry in particular, however, there seems to be a predilection for unqualified people who want to participate in the buying function.

For this reason, it is important to clearly define the purchasing responsibility and then carefully limit the number of people who are allowed to execute this responsibility. There should be no chance for nonpurchasing people to assume a purchasing role at any time. Allowing unqualified people to do so not only detracts from the professionalism of the purchasing job, but it also shows inconsistent abilities and skills to the supplier community, who will be very quick to take advantage of an unskilled purchaser.

While this problem may be minor in many of the individual restaurant operations, it can assume very significant proportions in the large chain. Certain suppliers have been known to encourage agreements from people in different areas of the business, assuming that if they avoid the purchasing department, they may be better able to impress the operations side of the business with the attractiveness or usefulness of their product. Generally speaking, a company with a well-structured and efficiently operated procurement function will terminate business relationships with such suppliers.

CONSIDERATIONS IN PURCHASING ORGANIZATION

Geography or Commodity?

In the larger restaurant chain, there may be up to a dozen or more people involved in the purchasing function. Usually these individuals have purchasing responsibility assigned to them on either a geographic or a commodity basis. In the case where responsibility is assigned on a commodity basis, one individual is usually held responsible for the procurement of similar type items. One person may be responsible for all meat procurement, another for all canned and dried groceries, and another for paper goods and operating supplies.

In my experience, a company that organizes its purchasing responsibility along commodity lines tends to develop the most efficient procurement methods. The reason for this is fundamental. The more time an individual devotes to a particular group of items, the greater his proficiency in buying those items. A buyer with assigned responsibility for purchasing fifty items can learn each of those fifty markets in greater detail than a buyer who has responsibility for three hundred items. This greater in-depth knowledge of each market will often help the buyer anticipate market trends, develop additional sources of supply that might not ordinarily be considered as potential vendors, and have a better feel for product substitution and/or specification modifications.

Obviously, the degree to which an organization can divide procurement responsibility along commodity lines will be directly related to the overall size of the operation, the degree of centralization of the procurement function, and the geographic dispersement of the individual units within the corporation. In the case of the individual operation or small group of restaurants owned by one person, such specialization is not usually affordable.

Centralization

Another important consideration in purchasing is centralization, which provides distinct advantages over a decentralized system. First and foremost, it increases the firm's ability to concentrate its purchase volume for an item or group of similar items that may be purchased from one supplier. One of the nation's largest restaurant chains presently has a decentralized procurement function. This means that local operations and purchasing personnel in district offices around the country are executing their own individual procurement programs without any thought of consolidating their identical purchases with their brother locations in other parts of the country. Not only are they failing to obtain maximum efficiency by segmenting their purchasing volume, but possibly even more important, they are engaged in highly duplicative purchasing efforts wherein anywhere from four to ten buyers are spending time negotiating the purchase of the same item. The only difference is the point of delivery. Consider how much more efficient it would be for one buyer to have total national responsibility for the procurement of that particular item, be it sugar packets, ketchup, or cleaning supplies, and thus save the time of the other buyers who could be devoting their energies to other products.

Major suppliers to the restaurant industry will frequently explain the special pricing which they offer to those large, national chains by saying that they are simply passing on to the buyer the savings which the supplier realizes as a result of having to make only one sales call on the buyer. The same rationale applies to the purchasing side. The fewer sales calls a purchasing department has made on its buyers, the less the expenses will be. Just as vendors have a goal of focusing their sales attention on one key decision maker in each chain, the chains themselves should aim at focusing their buying authority on one individual for each item purchased.

PURCHASING COOPERATIVES

No examination of potential purchasing structures would be complete without a brief consideration of purchasing cooperatives. Most of us know about cooperative buying organizations in the hardware, grocery, retail drug, and dairy industries. In recent years a number of buying cooperatives have sprung up in the restaurant industry, and in most cases they have been unqualified failures. The basic rationale behind the purchasing cooperative in any industry is to concentrate purchase volume and thereby receive better pricing and service. Unfortunately, while this theory is fine on paper, it doesn't work in reality for the very simple reason that most cooperatives are saddled with individual members who each sincerely believe that his ideas are better than those of any other member of the cooperative.

If the people participating in the co-op recognize what a well-run cooperative can do, and if they are willing to allow the assigned individuals to carry out their task without interference, a buying co-op can be a great success. The potential value of the buying co-op to the individual operator can be enormous. It is not unreasonable to expect price reductions on certain items of as much as ten to fifteen percent as a result of a well-established and properly executed co-op buying program.

For any co-op to succeed, however, it is an absolute prerequisite that a carefully detailed set of guidelines be established not only for the members, but for the vendors who will be doing business with the co-op. Both sides must clearly understand these ground rules and must pledge to abide by them if the co-op is to succeed. Figure 5 is a sample of the principles set down by a very successful cooperative buying operation in another industry. Although the industry is different, the basic principles are the same and can be used as general guidelines for any group of restaurant operators wishing to form such a cooperative.

The other prerequisite for success is to clearly identify one individual who will have the ultimate decision-making authority for the co-op. If this is not done, there is very little chance that the co-op will exist harmoniously and satisfy all the members.

Another way of insuring the success of a cooperative buying operation is to charge each member a nominal fee for participation in the organization. Although this is rarely done, it can help each member to recognize that the co-op does have certain operating expenses, but that it can return to him in savings many times more than the cost of his participation.

The financing of most buying cooperatives comes from suppliers who provide discounts or rebates on all purchases made by the cooperative. This is a short-sighted method of financing any buying cooperative other than those which service nonprofit organizations such as hospitals, schools, religious institutions, and private clubs. The minute a buying cooperative serving profit-making businesses becomes involved in rebates from the suppliers, the seeds of member discontent are sewn throughout the organization. The purpose of a cooperative should be to bring in the lowest net cost consistent with quality

Rules of the Cooperative

1. All members recognize that the co-op exists for the greater good of *all* the members.
2. All members understand that the primary purpose of the co-op is to pool the purchasing requirements of the members in order to maximize purchasing leverage for the good of all.
3. All members agree to purchase their requirements through the co-op at all times.
4. All members agree to provide information as to product quality, specifications, yield, etc., to the co-op at any time upon request.
5. Members understand that in order to perform at maximum efficiency, the co-op must have product requirement information well in advance of procurement dates. Consequently they agree to provide quarterly and monthly forecasts of product requirements by item to the co-op on a regularly scheduled basis.
6. All volume refunds due the co-op will be paid to it for equal distribution to all the members. No member shall accept any direct rebate, refund or other consideration from any vendor doing business with the co-op.
7. The co-op will provide a quarterly accounting of all its activities to its members.
8. The members are encouraged to make recommendations for improved co-op performance to the directors of the co-op at any time.

Figure 5

that can be developed for the members of the cooperative. If these funds are being channeled back to the cooperative without provision for total redistribution to all the members, then certain members are bound to feel that they are not receiving the full value of the cooperative's services. Once this discontent gets started in a buying cooperative, member dissatisfaction will cause its ultimate dissolution.

Perhaps I can best sum up my attitudes on purchasing cooperatives in the restaurant industry by saying that 1) they are a very sound device, and 2) they can contribute great results *if* they are properly organized and have their operating principles clearly detailed in writing for all members and suppliers.

Chapter 2 Questions

1. Why is it important that limits on buying authority be established for each buyer?

2. Why is it strategically unsound for a supplier to attempt to bypass the purchasing department in making a sale?

3. What are the reasons why a multiunit food service operation might want to concentrate the purchase responsibility for a specific item or group of items with one buyer?

4. List the reasons why purchasing co-ops frequently fail to achieve their goals.

5. Discuss the steps you would take to form a purchasing cooperative in your area.

3

Source Selection

WHAT IS SOURCE SELECTION?

A key ingredient in the effectiveness of any purchasing program is the process of source selection to set up supply arrangements. *Source selection* means picking the best qualified vendor to satisfy the buyer's particular needs. This is one of the most overlooked areas in the purchasing profession. Buyers will tend to assume that all sources are pretty much the same for a given item, and aside from minor variations in price, it really doesn't matter which source they use. Nothing could be further from the truth.

STEPS IN SOURCE SELECTION

Source selection should involve a series of steps before price is even considered. The first and most important is obtaining information on the past performance of a particular vendor. If the vendor approaches you with a request for consideration of his products and services, you should begin by asking the vendor to supply the names of other buyers with whom he has an ongoing relationship. This should include the name of both the company and the individual with whom he conducts his business. You should make it a point to contact one or more references and check out the supplier prior to placing your first order with him. This is particularly important if you move into a new geographical area where you do not have any supplier familiarity. Such would be the case of a food service company taking a college feeding contract in a new area.

Ask Questions

In checking out a supplier you should ask the following questions:

- Is his firm reliable?
- Does he make deliveries as promised?
- What is his out of stock/back order record?
- Does the firm provide accurate counts of product shipped as compared with product ordered?
- Are the prices quoted by this firm competitive?
- For what period of time is this vendor willing to hold his price?
- Does he have any minimum order requirements?
- Are there any days on which he will not make a delivery?
- Does he have an emergency delivery service?
- Is the quality of his product consistent?
- Are his employees cooperative and willing to respond to the customer's needs?
- Does he offer any ancillary services such as menu planning, new product development, equipment, etc.
- Is he willing to enter into long term contracts where price and supply are guaranteed for extended periods?

While this listing may appear excessive, try to remember that once you have selected a supplier, you must stay with that suppleir until you choose another. There is no point in a careless selection of supplier. Take the time at the outset to carefully evaluate a supplier so you can be sure that he has the type of organization you wish to deal with.

Meet with the Supplier

After this checking process has been completed, you should ask the supplier to meet with you to discuss your specific needs. This initial meeting should be attended by a decision maker in the vendor's company. Do not be satisfied with a brief meeting with a route salesman who may not have the authority to make any of the key decisions which could very well effect your relationship with his particular company.

For example, many of the major institutional distributors have very strict rules regarding minimum order quantity. A route salesman in his enthusiasm to sign on a new account may not properly emphasize this minimum order requirement to the buyer. Having selected this particular vendor, the buyer may begin to place orders only to find that the order quantity does not come up to the minimum requirements. If you consider the time wasted in situations like this, you can clearly understand the reason why these questions should be resolved early in the game.

Keep Your Options Open

The next step in the selection process is to place what we shall refer to as a trial order with the vendor. You should recognize that during the first few orders you give the vendor, he will be on his "best behavior" and will attempt to service you with utmost efficiency. It may well be a half dozen or more orders later before you will receive a true picture of the vendor's ongoing capability. For this reason, be sure to keep your options open by dealing with a number of vendors simultaneously until you are confident that you have selected the one in each product area who is the most reliable. This process of vendor selection should be an ongoing exercise even in the well-established company that feels it has thoroughly researched the market.

Any buyer who states that he has developed a sufficient number of vendors and is not interested in considering any additional suppliers is extremely short sighted. Supplier selection should be an ongoing process of continually upgrading the vendors from whom you purchase. Companies are constantly coming into or leaving the market place. With the many new developments in the restaurant industry over just the past five years (microwave ovens, steak items that have been needled or enzyme-treated for tenderness, prepared frozen entrees), you simply cannot afford to have a static inventory of suppliers. You must be constantly on the lookout for new and improved sources of supply at the same time as you work with those suppliers who have shown a desire to grow with you.

COMPETITIVE BIDDING

Once supplier selection has been fairly well completed, you can begin to concentrate on the all-important area of competitive bidding. Probably no term in the purchasing lexicon is less understood than the expression *competitive bidding*. Competitive bidding simply means obtaining each vendor's best offer for a predetermined quality and quantity of merchandise, and then awarding the purchase order to that vendor who submits the lowest bid. Naturally, one must take into account the reliability, quality of delivery, billing terms, and product quality in determining whether a series of bids are truly comparable.

The more the buyer can do to make all bids truly comparable, the better opportunity he will have for developing truly competitive bids. The best way to make these bids truly comparable is to spell out in writing precisely what you are requesting when you send out your invitations to bid. You should include detailed product specifications, unless the supplier is so totally familiar with the product being purchased that sending specifications would be a waste of time. This should state all requirements relative to delivery, billing, shipping schedules, delivery arrangements, credit terms, etc. It should also indicate a closing date for all bids. You should instruct each prospective supplier to contact you immediately if he has any questions about the specifications.

Once all the bids are in, you are in a position to evaluate them and award the contract to the lowest bidder. Probably the most grievous mistake that any buyer can make is to reveal the nature of a bid submitted by one potential vendor to a representative of a competitive firm. Once a buyer lets a vendor know where his competition stands, he has effectively destroyed the usefulness of the competitive bidding system to his company. Vendors respect buyers of integrity. They don't mind competing under a straight-forward competitive bidding system, as long as all vendors are treated equally. The minute a vendor has any indication that favoritism is being shown to one of his competitors, he will quickly back away from the competitive bidding system. Even the vendor who is so favored by the disclosure of a competitor's bid quickly loses respect for the buyer and begins to take advantage of his weakness in future transactions. The best rule of thumb for you to follow once you set up a true competitive bidding system is never to violate the basic principle of it.

WHEN TO USE COMPETITIVE BIDDING

One question often asked in the restaurant industry is, "When should a buyer rely on competitive bidding, and when should he just order his needs from the most convenient supplier?" As a general rule, you should avoid competitive bidding only when the potential amount you can save through the competitive bidding process is less than the cost equivalent of the time required to implement it.

While it is difficult to draw a specific dollar value or order size guideline to follow, your own common sense will usually be a good indication of whether the items being purchased, and the potential dollar savings to be derived from competitive bidding, justify the expenditure of time and effort (telephone, mail contact expense, etc.) that a competitive bidding process requires. Certainly the competitive bidding technique should be utilized anytime the dollar value of a prospective purchase exceeds $500. In fact, there may be many companies who choose to set an even lower purchase value in this regard.

Suppose a particular restaurant has a weekly requirement for three crates of lettuce. Past experience with the competitive bidding process indicates that the maximum saving as a result of competitive bidding will be 75¢ per crate or $2.25 per week. With these figures in mind, the buyer should then evaluate whether the time required to obtain the necessary competitive bids on a weekly basis is worth the potential savings. In situations where the weekly volume and potential savings are as slim as this, it might be far more effective for the buyer to attempt to negotiate an agreement with the vendor who has been the low bidder in the past something like this:

Buyer: I am prepared to give you all my produce business for the next four weeks (perhaps he would make it eight weeks or more) if you will agree to hold the current price on the various produce items which you are selling me at that level.

Vendor: Well, if I can be assured of your total volume over this period of time, I think I would be prepared to guarantee the current price for that period.

If an arrangement of this type can be worked out, both the buyer and the seller profit from it. The buyer has the advantage of knowing that his price (apparently one which he felt was competitive, or he would not have initiated the arrangement in the first place) will be fixed for a specific period of time. The vendor benefits by knowing that he has this particular customer's business locked up for a fixed period of time, and can thus devote his sales efforts to other customers and plan his ordering and inventory procedures more effectively because he knows exactly what this customer's business will be. There are many times when this type of arrangement can work very well. However, you must know your potential savings from previous experience with competitive bidding before you enter into this type of agreement. Otherwise, you are in no position to evaluate and compare the relative merits of each process.

You should also avoid competitive bidding when you request a particular product or sales service which is not available from all vendors. For example, if a buyer requires a particular food item for a special menu and knows that it is available from only one purveyor in the immediate area, he is wasting his time and the other vendors' time by asking them to submit quotations on the item. Or, if the buyer requires delivery of a particular item at 6 o'clock on a Sunday evening and knows that all but one of his vendors refuse to make such deliveries at that time, there is no point in getting competitive bids. The individual circumstances of each buying opportunity will probably be the best guideline to follow in determining whether or not to use the competitive bidding process.

When a particular product is available from only one purveyor, competitive bidding cannot take place. If the use of such unique products (perhaps in brand name only) provides an increased operating margin or operating efficiency, then the potential savings from competitive bidding can be overlooked. However, under any other situations, you should remember that if a product is specified in such a way that no competitive comparison can be made, then the chance of ever recognizing potential savings is lost. Hence, wherever possible, avoid specifying products which cannot be subjected to some sort of competitive analysis.

You should also realize that the moment you decide to use a product that is available from only one purveyor (for example, a specific brand name piece of equipment), the vendor knows immediately that he has no price competition. Without competition, the vendor is free to charge whatever price the market will bear.

During the course of my purchasing experience, I have seen many, many situations in which a product previously available from a single source was finally placed on a multiple source basis. Immediately significant price reductions followed, not only from the additional suppliers, but more importantly, from the original vendor who was then forced to meet a competitive price situation.

The magnitude of some of these price reductions was truly startling. I have personally witnessed a number of reductions of 25% or more, simply as the result of competitive bidding. On the basis of these situations, I would urge any buyer who requires items which are available only from one source of supply either to search the marketplace for additional sources, or to modify existing specifications to accept merchandise from additional potential suppliers.

In the chain buying operation, a good rule of thumb is to state that any purchase with a total value in excess of $500 must be submitted to the competitive bidding process unless one of the conditions outlined above clearly governs. If one of these conditions does govern, you should seriously consider eliminating the particular circumstances blocking your ability to get competitive bids.

Repetitive purchases under $500 per buying incident may be excluded from competitive bidding, but you should certainly try to negotiate some sort of long term purchase arrangement with a particular vendor. Such things as supply and maintenance items lend themselves particularly well to this type of arrangement.

VENDOR RELATIONS

Another area of frequent discussion and sometimes disagreement is the broad subject of vendor relations. Good relations with vendors can often be the most important ingredient in a successful purchasing program. However, it is important to distinguish between good relations that result from acquiescence on the part of the buyer and the good relations which are built by a fair, unbiased, intelligent, and demanding relationship with vendors. The former creates a false feeling of success, since the buyer is only kidding himself and his company. His good relationships with his vendors would quickly deteriorate if he did not always do things their way. In the latter case, however, the buyer forges a relationship based on mutual respect and trust between himself and his vendors. It has been my experience that a vendor is more likely to respect and work harder for a buyer who is tough but fair than he is for a fellow who is willing to go along with whatever he suggests.

It is important for both buyers and their superiors to recognize that vendors are not adversaries. In fact, the degree to which they can become loyal, reliable, and trustworthy allies will have an important impact on the efficiency of your operation. An excellent example of this occurred during the widespread supply shortages of 1973 and early 1974. Those firms who had good supplier relationships and who treated their vendors with respect and confidence were generally the last ones to find themselves out of stock on critical items. On the other hand, those firms who abused their suppliers or made unreasonable demands on them were quickly shut off when supplies became tight and vendors had to chose which of their customers they would continue to service without interruption.

One of a buyer's most important obligations is to be sure that he and his colleagues treat their suppliers with fairness and respect. Non-purchasing people are particularly prone to consider vendors as little more than doormats to be walked upon. Buyers should realize that vendors are human beings too, and have the same needs for personal respect and dignity as buyers do. This is certainly an appropriate area for the buyer to remind himself of the application of the golden rule, which will enhance any buyer-vendor relationship. Good vendor relations do not always come easily, but they are fundamental for any buyer who hopes to achieve maximum efficiency in his purchasing responsibility.

SPECIAL SERVICES

A problem most buyers confront at some time is determining the limits on the special services they should require of their suppliers. This question can be answered in several ways. First, a buyer should not hesitate to ask a vendor to provide any service that is generally available from other vendors. Second, he should not hesitate to ask for any service that will enhance the value of the vendor's product in his operation so long as the vendor is not asked to incur unreasonable costs in providing that service, or so long as the buyer underwrites the additional cost that is incurred.

For example, the owners of a seafood house may base its reputation for fresh seafood so much around daily deliveries that they feel that it necessary for their fresh fish supplier to make a Sunday delivery. If there are other vendors willing to provide this service at no charge, there is no reason why the seafood house should not ask their present vendor to perform a similar service.

A buyer should also feel free to ask his vendor for the results of bacterial testing on the vendor's product, chemical analyses of random samples, or random samples of the product for testing in the buyer's quality control laboratory. These requests are certainly in keeping with the buyer's desire to provide optimum quality in the product he is purchasing.

There are several services, however, which the buyer should *not* request. Among them are:

- Free goods of any kind other than an initial sample prior to purchasing from a given vendor.
- Unreasonably small deliveries required frequently.
- Any type of personal service such as gratuities, free products for the buyer's personal consumption, entertainment, etc.
- Special consideration with regard to payment terms, such as discount, or any type of rebate or refund not in keeping with generally accepted trade practice.

If a buyer does request any of these special services, he should recognize that he not only compromises his own integrity and the integrity of his firm, but he also creates a situation in which the vendor himself is forced to cover the additional cost of these services in the initial price charged for the merchandise. Always remember that the vendor is in business to make a reasonable profit, just as the food service company is. To expect the vendor to perform services which are not in keeping with industry tradition and trade practice only means that ultimately the buyer will pay for these special services in the price charged for the product he is purchasing. Although it is difficult to anticipate every possible request that may arise, the buyer should operate on the basis that if he has any doubts about the propriety of the request he is making, then he should not make that request.

Chapter 3 Questions

1. What questions should the buyer ask in qualifying a potential new source of supply to do business with his company?

2. What can the buyer expect to learn from a trial order placed with a new potential vendor, and what should he be wary of in evaluating the trial order?

3. Why should a buyer always be on the alert for new sources of supply?

4. How do you define the process of competitive bidding?

5. Under what circumstances should a buyer not rely on competitive bidding in his procurement activity?

6. What steps should a buyer take to build good vendor relations?

4

Price Considerations

DETERMINING THE WORTH OF AN ITEM

After the buyer has completed his preliminary vendor selection and has established the proper ground rules for vendor approval and competitive bidding practices, he is then in a position to concentrate on an area that enters into virtually every purchasing transaction: the pricing considerations. A fundamental question that has mystified purchasing people for centuries has been, "How does one determine what is the best price?" A learned writer in 42 B.C. once said, "Everything is worth what its purchaser will pay for it." While this hypothesis may appear somewhat simplistic, it contains a fundamental truth of purchasing.

Another way of describing the *worth* of an item is its value to a buyer. We have referred earlier to the price/value relationship as a key point in the purchasing framework. In this particular case, *worth* can be described as *value* or *utility*. A pound of shrimp, a case of lettuce, or a dozen coffee cups all have certain upward limits on their worth. When shrimp gets above a certain price, the restaurateur either removes it from his menu or makes it available at an additional charge. If a dozen coffee cups suddenly rise to a point where the operator feels the price is unreasonable, he immediately begins looking at substitute products made from glass or plastic, rather than ceramic materials. As for lettuce, while the operator may be forced to continue buying it at a price which he considers excessive, he will reduce his usage per portion and may adjust his menu price to reflect his higher cost.

THE BASIC LAWS OF SUPPLY AND DEMAND

Generally, however, the price of any item is determined by the basic law of supply and demand. A buyer for a restaurant operation, be it large or small, should always try to use the laws of supply and demand to his own advantage. When he sees the supply of a given item grow in proportion to its demand, he should presume that prices will fall, and should not hesitate to tell his vendors so. On the other hand, when he sees the supply of a given item dwindle in relationship to the demand for that item (as we have seen all too frequently in the last few years), he should take whatever steps he can to lessen his need for that particular item.

The rapid increase in the price of fresh lobster over the past three years has caused some of the most prestigious seafood restaurants in the United States to either eliminate lobster from their menu entirely, or to offer it at a fairly steep surcharge with a clear statement on the menu explaining why the surcharge is necessary. Many other seafood houses have chosen the route of substitution, downplaying the prominence of fresh lobster on the menu and replacing it with a more attractively priced offering of "lobster tails." (Many of us are aware that these "lobster tails" are, in fact, not even lobster, but rather cray fish tails from South American waters. However, their general popularity in the United States has resulted in their being commonly described as "lobster tails.")

In many ways the restaurant industry is unique in its ability to substitute or remove entirely those items which have suddenly become excessively scarce or unreasonably high priced. Most manufacturing industries (and I believe the restaurant business should be classified as a manufacturing industry, at least on the food preparation side) do not have the luxury of this type of flexibility. Once they introduce a specific product or product line, it is a long-time, consuming process to modify it.

If we are to look at the automobile or home appliance industries, for example, we can see that even though a particular component part in one of their major product lines might suddenly increase in price, it is difficult for the manufacturer to immediately raise the price or to substitute another part for the component part. The nature of their manufacturing planning, distribution, and consumer pricing activities makes it extremely difficult to have a short reaction time when a sudden unexpected price increase or product shortage occurs.

However, in the restaurant industry the only limit on a change to reflect a price increase or a product shortage is the speed with which an operator can implement a menu change. Admittedly, this change is a lot easier in the single unit operation, which may simply cross out a particular offering on the menu, than it would be in a multiunit food service organization where thousands of menus have to be reprinted when changes occur. Nevertheless, even considering the reprinting time, even the largest restaurants can implement basic changes with greater ease, flexibility, and rapidity than almost any other industry.

This inherent flexibility is both a tremendous advantage and an important responsibility for the buyer. Usually the buyer is the first one to spot a supply/demand trend, so it is his responsibility to immediately identify the situation for other members of his management.

In the larger chains some of the more sophisticated purchasing departments prepare regular twelve month forecasts on the availability of key raw material items. These forecasts, as shown in Figure 6, predict both the availability of the product in terms of pounds per month, and the price fluctuations which are anticipated. Usually these forecasts should be revised every 90 days, along with the preparation of a new forecast for the next twelve months at that time. These forecasts enable the operations people in the large chains not only to plan their menus, but also to provide "early warning signals" of unusually attractive price/supply situations which can be used in special advertising and promotion plans. These activities often give a particular chain substantial advantage over its competition.

For example, one major sit down restaurant chain advertises "nightly specials," where one item is broadly featured at a special promotion price. Since these promotions have to be planned six to nine months in advance, forecasts received from the purchasing department are a critical factor in setting them up. Thus a special purchasing forecast regarding the price and availability of, say, turkey in the next

PRICE/SUPPLY FORECASTS

As of 1/1/76
For Period Jan-Dec 1976

Item	Annual Requirement (Pounds)	JAN-MAR Supply	JAN-MAR Avg. Price	APR-JUNE Supply	APR-JUNE Avg. Price	JULY-SEPT Supply	JULY-SEPT Avg. Price	OCT-DEC Supply	OCT-DEC Avg. Price
Shoe String Potatoes	20,000,000	Unlimited	28¢/lb	Tight	29¢	Tight	29¢	Unlimited	28¢
Cod Blocks	5,000,000	Adequate	78¢	Tight (1,000,000 lb)	87¢	Tight (1,000,000 lb)	94¢	Scarce (500,000 lb)	99¢
Scallops	1,000,000	Tight (70,000 lb)	$2.60	Scarce (45,000 lb)	$2.80	Adequate	$2.50	Adequate	$2.50
Imported Boneless Beef	10,000,000	Unlimited	75¢	Adequate	89¢	Adequate	93¢	Unlimited	79¢
Broilers	4,000,000	Unlimited	44¢	Adequate	49¢	Adequate	54¢	Unlimited	46¢

NOTE: Where no poundage amount is shown, available supply will more than cover needs.

Figure 6

nine months can play a major role in deciding to use turkey and in establishing a promotion for it in the chain's restaurants.

KNOW THE MARKET CONDITIONS OF THE MOMENT

The key point to remember here is that the supply/demand relationship constantly changes for most of the items purchased for a restaurant operation. By being aware of market conditions of the moment, and by using this knowledge to negotiate with suppliers, the sharp buyer can substantially improve the price/value relationships he delivers for his company.

Vendors are also aware of these changes in the supply/demand cycle, and use them for their own operating efficiency to improve their profit margins. For example, many of the major institutional distributors who handle frozen vegetables in quantity will buy their yearly anticipated requirements at the time of harvest (commonly referred to as *new pack time*). They know from past experience that prices tend to be lower at this time because of the additional quantities of product immediately available, which must be moved by the growers and processors within a relatively short period of time. By attempting to make their purchases at this time, they are actually utilizing the supply/demand cycle to their best advantage. Since demand for a frozen vegetable (peas, carrots, corn, string beans, etc.) tends to be relatively constant throughout the year, the supply of these products at the harvest time substantially outweighs the demand, and thereby results in lower prices.

If the large institutional distributor recognizes this trend and also negotiates his annual purchase requirements at this time, he will usually obtain a lower price on his requirements than he would if he were to buy $\frac{1}{12}$ of his needs in each of the twelve months of the calendar year. Institutional distributors admit that a large part of their profit margins result from sound purchasing practices.

The buyer for any restaurant operation should also use such techniques in his own operation. Obviously, this is easier for large chains that have sufficient purchasing leverage to negotiate substantial volume contracts than for the small operator. However, even the individual or small multi-unit operator can take advantage of these known supply/demand cycles to enhance his own purchasing effectiveness.

TIMING YOUR PURCHASES

Now that we have discussed the basic supply/demand cycles, let us consider the question of timing of purchases. An anonymous wise man once said, "Timing is everything in life." While this generalization may or may not bear up in other areas, it is certainly of paramount importance in the purchasing profession. A buyer who is able to develop the technique for proper timing on his purchases can frequently save five to ten percent on his annual costs. Naturally, this percentage fluctuates, depending upon the volatility and the range of the price movement for each item during a given year. However, buyers who watch a particular group of commodity items on a regular basis tend to develop a type of "sixth sense" as to when a price move is about to occur, so that they can either implement or postpone their purchases, depending on what type of price activity they anticipate.

PRICE CYCLES

As in the case of frozen vegetables, most agricultural commodities, as well as most animal proteins, exhibit annual price cycles. Fruit, vegetable, grain, and produce cycles tend to coincide with their harvest schedules. The annual price move of corn, tomatoes, frozen peas, or frozen strawberries, for example, is generally lowest thirty days before and after the peak of the harvest season. From that point on, the price gradually increases until it reaches a high for the year sometime between five to ten months after the harvest period. After this point and until the next harvest, the prices move downward in anticipation of the new harvest cycle.

Figure 7 demonstrates this type of price movement over a twelve month period. Naturally, unexpected developments such as severe weather problems, crop failures due to blight or insect activity, or sudden increases in demand (as in the case of the Soviet wheat purchases several years ago) will throw the cycles totally off. However, for most years, assuming that none of these special factors occur, you should expect the natural price cycle described above.

In the case of the animal proteins, you can identify a similar price cycle. This cycle is related directly to the peaks of slaughter which occur throughout the calendar year. For example, the peak slaughter period for beef cattle normally occurs during the months of October and November. There is then a secondary heavy slaughter period generally in March and April. If you look again at Figure 7 you will note the price valleys which occur twice a year and coincide with these peak slaughter periods. Once you become aware of these cyclical movements, you can then time your purchasing activity to take maximum advantage of them.

ARRANGEMENTS WITH PURVEYORS

Obviously, most buyers will not be able to purchase and store their year's requirements for a given item once or even twice a year. However, there are many opportunities available for a buyer to price his merchandise once or twice a year, and then enter into an arrangement with the purveyor to have him carry the product and bill the buyer for it at the time of shipment. These arrangements normally call for the buyer to pay a monthly carrying charge, which covers the cost of storage, insurance, and interest on the vendor's money.

In the egg business the customary carrying charge on frozen egg products is $4/10$ of a cent per pound per month. This means quite simply that if the buyer is successful in pricing his requirements at or near the annual low of the market; and if he expects to see a price fluctuation during the next ten to twelve months of anywhere from ten to fifteen cents per pound (not at all unusual in the frozen egg market), then he can well afford to pay the carrying charges of $4/10$ of a cent per pound per month, or 4.8 cents per pound per year, to have his vendor carry the inventory for him.

In actuality his average carrying cost, assuming that he will withdraw approximately equal quantities of the product every month for the twelve month period, will amount to only 2.4 cents per pound ($4/10$ of a cent per pound per month times twelve months, divided by two equals 2.4 cents per pound average carrying charge). When a buyer has a price fixing opportunity available to him at such a modest carrying charge for a commodity which is known to have fairly wide price fluctuations, he should be very quick to take advantage of this opportunity.

There is no general rule as to the availability of such arrangements. While these arrangements are fairly common for most frozen food, canned, or dried items, they are practically unavailable for most

Figure 7   Typical seasonal price movements

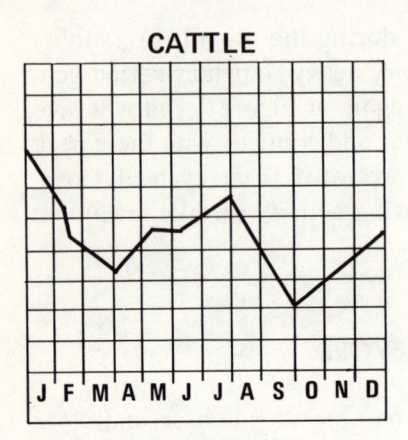

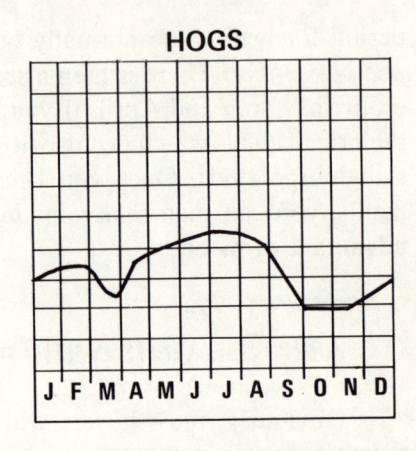

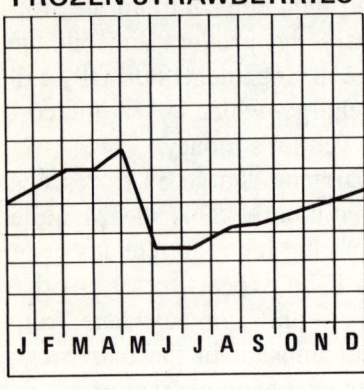

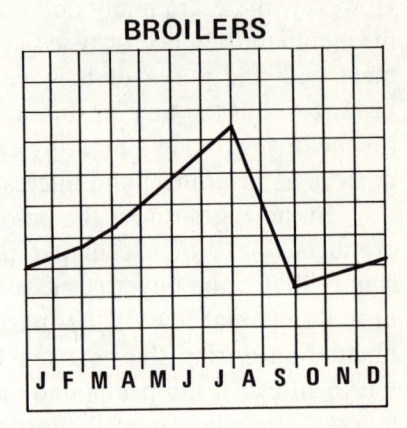

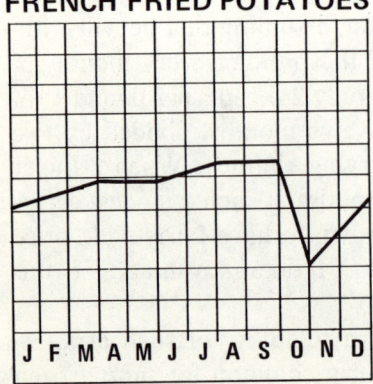

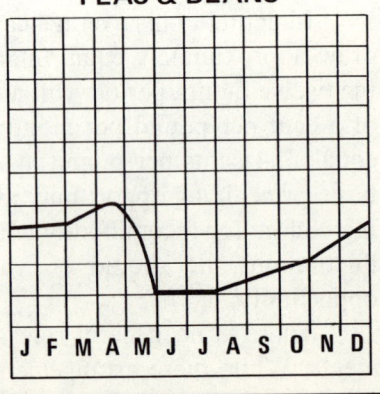

These graphs are intended to demonstrate the pattern of price movements in these commodities over a typical 12-month period. The absolute dollar value at any point in time is not shown on these charts because the primary purpose is to demonstrate the seasonality of their typical price movements.

Note that cattle and hog prices tend to move together seasonally with price lows coinciding with the two peak slaughter (harvest) periods each year: February-March and October-November.

Interestingly enough, however, broiler prices follow a different pattern for two reasons: 1) it only takes 12 weeks to grow a broiler-size chicken, so there are continuous harvest seasons year round, and 2) there is a sharp increase in demand for broilers during the summer barbecue season.

In the case of the vegetables, seasonal low prices are directly tied to harvest periods: potatoes in late October, strawberries in late May and early June, and peas and beans in June and July.

Each commodity has its own distinct seasonal price pattern. The sharp buyer can improve his performance by learning and using them to advantage.

fresh items. Even though a buyer may not be in a position to purchase large quantities of merchandise at a given time or to negotiate a carrying charge arrangement, he can still anticipate price movements and time his short-term purchase activity accordingly. While he may not be in a position to purchase a six month supply of a given item, for example, chances are he can purchase a four to six week supply of that same item without straining either his financial resources or his storage capabilities. In many cases, he will be able to negotiate a purchase arrangement with his vendor with the stipulation that deliveries be made over an extended period of time.

This is frequently a very effective way for a buyer to take advantage of a near-term anticipated price increase without committing capital or storage space to the product purchased. For example, if a restaurant requires thirty oven-ready ribs of beef each week, and the buyer anticipates that the price will be rising over the next four weeks, he might call his primary supplier and attempt to negotiate a contract for 180 oven-ready ribs to be delivered in weekly increments of thirty each over the next six-week period. If his relationships with his suppliers are sound, and if the supplier is anxious for business, he might very well agree to this arrangement.

PRICE DETERMINATION IN PURCHASE CONTRACTS

There are two common ways of approaching price determination in purchase contracts. One is to buy on a market price date-of-shipment basis. The other is to agree with the vendor on a fixed price to cover a specific period of time. There are advantages and disadvantages of both methods.

In the case of purchase on a market price date-of-shipment basis, the buyer is retaining the flexibility of paying whatever is the going price on the actual date that the merchandise is shipped to him. When setting up a contract of this type, the buyer usually anticipates a lower price and is therefore willing to take his chances on future price activity. He may also be in a situation where guaranteed supply is more important to him than price.

For example, suppose the buyer for a large seafood restaurant is contracting for supplies of fresh lobster. He may feel that it is more important to establish vendor contacts that will guarantee fresh supplies than it is to attempt to fix the price for any specific length of time. With a commodity like fresh lobster, the vendor will usually refuse to make any long-term commitment on price due to its extreme price volatility. The buyer might well figure that a supply commitment from the vendor is more important than a price commitment. Therefore, he will ask the vendor to give him an option to purchase a fixed number of lobsters each week at the current market price.

It is important to note the difference between a buyer receiving an option to buy from a vendor and a buyer making a firm quantity commitment to a vendor. The former alternative gives the buyer far more flexibility, for if his demand declines, he is under no obligation to exercise the option and take the quantity. However, if his demand stays at the level he projected, the vendor is under an obligation to give him the quantity optioned.

METHODS OF PRICE DETERMINATION

In determining price, there are several methods to consider. The most flexible is the market price date-of-shipment method. This method insures that the buyer will pay no more than the going market price. However, it also insures that he will buy at no less than the going market price. This assurance of always being "on the market" appeals to some people, although in reality the major benefits of this type of purchasing approach are the supply guarantee aspects of it.

A second kind of arrangement is the fixed contract price method of purchasing, whereby the buyer and seller negotiate a mutually acceptable price that will apply for a fixed period of time, regardless of market price movement during that time. While this arrangement provides the greatest opportunity for the buyer to use his price judgment skills, it also opens up the greatest risk and chance for error in determining price.

In using this approach the buyer identifies a specific quantity and quality of product he expects to consume over a specific period of time. This period of time may be as short as one week or as long as one year or more. The buyer and seller then negotiate the price and delivery terms. Once agreed upon, these terms become binding on both parties for the duration of the contract. If the buyer feels that market prices will rise during the period of the contract, it is obviously to his advantage to fix a price at or close to the current market levels. Conversely, if the seller believes that the price will drop during the contract period, it is to his advantage to confirm the contract at a price below the current level.

Even in a situation where the seller may feel the price will be rising during the contract period, it may be advantageous for him to fix the price at the current level if he has some means of protecting himself; for example, making certain that he in turn can guarantee his raw material price for the same period. This approach will be detailed further in the next chapter.

The greatest risk in the fixed price method of procurement is that the buyer will agree to a price of an item whose market value declines during the period of his contract. Although in this time of generally rising prices there would seem to be little risk in this regard, we must remember that there are definite up and down cyclical movements even within an overall price rise. Although the price of frozen vegetables, for example, may rise from year to year, harvest influenced cycles of price weakness still exist, and a buyer who has made a long-term commitment on vegetables three to five months prior to a harvest period could very well find himself paying a substantially higher price than he would if he had waited until the peak of the harvest season.

Generally speaking, the longer the period for which the buyer is willing to make a commitment, the more willing the vendor will be to provide price concessions. This is because the longer the vendor can "tie up" that buyer under a fixed price purchase contract, the longer he is assured of keeping that buyer's business and not losing it to another vendor. Since every vendor must recognize his selling expense as one of his costs of doing business, any long-term contract with price concessions included would reduce his future selling expense.

CONTRACT VARIATIONS

A variation which combines the best features of both the market price date-of-shipment approach and long-term fixed price contract buying can sometimes be worked out by large chains. This involves entering into a long-term fixed price contract with a vendor with the understanding that if the market price should drop below a certain level during the period of the contract, either the price will be reopened for further negotiation or a new, lower market price will automatically be put into effect.

For example, suppose a nationwide fast food chain, Hamburger Emporiums, Ltd., enters into a supply contract for five million pounds each of cheese slices and of French fried potatoes. In both contracts the buyer for Hamburger Emporiums, Ltd. agrees to a fixed price for a twelve-month period: $1.03 per pound for cheese slices, cut 24 slices to the pound, and 27¢ per pound for shoe string French fries. Both contracts cover a one-year period and stipulate that if, on the first of each following month after the date of contract execution, the market price for the item has fallen 5% below the agreed upon contract price, the new market price shall prevail for the next thirty days. At the end of that thirty-day period, the original contract price will go back into effect if the market price has risen above it, and if it has not, then the current market price will continue to prevail, with adjustments occurring on the first of each succeeding month.

Contracts of this type are not normally established for small operations with only modest requirements. However, in the case of a major chain, they can provide excellent price protection and price flexibility. Frequently, such a contract requires that the buyer initiate suggestions for contracts of this type, since the supplier normally prefers not to provide such flexibility to the buyer. However, the buyer should not hesitate to show a creative approach to large quantity procurement by suggesting variations of this type to the vendor.

Another common method of establishing purchase price levels is to utilize a recognized market price quotation sheet such as the Urner-Barry Report covering the butter and egg markets, or the Yellow Sheet published by the National Provisioner covering the cattle and pork markets. If prices are to be tied to a market quotation sheet, the procedure usually follows the same pattern. The buyer and seller agree on a fixed quantity and quality of product and agree to price it at a fixed amount over or under the market quotation sheet price for a specific item. Thus, if the market for Grade A medium white eggs is 60¢ per dozen, Chicago basis, the buyer and seller might agree to price each week's delivery at 3¢ per dozen over the price quoted every Friday. Similarly, a buyer of fresh ham might agree with his vendor to price the week's supply of fresh hams at 2¢ per pound under the Yellow Sheet quotation for that size ham as of Thursday of the week preceding the one in which the product was to be shipped. There is no set rule for establishing these types of price pegging formulas. Each one is worked out to the mutual satisfaction of the buyer and the seller and has as its main purpose guaranteeing a continuity of supply to the buyer at a price which is fair to both buyer and seller.

Unfortunately, there is a necessary word of caution which must be recognized when using market price sheets as a basis for establishing purchase and sale prices. There have been situations where market price sheets have been manipulated by sellers wishing to establish an artificially high price to be used in pegging their sale price to customers. Although difficult to prove, this artificial manipulation usually works in the following way. A large beef processor with a number of market price sheet type sales arrangements might call another processor the day on which the sheet price is to be used as the basis for establishing a sales price to his customers. He then deliberately purchases a small quantity of the specific item at a price several cents per pound over the going market. Since this is regarded by the selling processor as a legitimate sale, he reports it to the price reporting service, who in turn uses that particular price as the basis for establishing the market for that given day. In reality, the small quantity sold at the artificially high price level is not the true market, but since it is included in the market quotation price sheet, it then becomes the basis on which the buying processor's sales to all his customers are consummated. Since unethical processors have resorted to this type of artificial market price stimulation, the buyer should beware of the possibility of its developing.

A variation on using market price quotation sheets as the basis on which to apply purchase price formulas is the commonly used practice of establishing a formula which relates to the basic cost of the raw material going into the product which the buyer is actually purchasing. For example, the cost of French fried potatoes might be tied to the field price of raw potatoes; the price of one pound packages of frozen sliced strawberries, to the field price of strawberries; the price of three-ounce flounder fillets, to the boat price for whole flounder; and the price of coffee tied to the F.O.B. Colombia price of green coffee beans. This type of pricing formula tends to be most often utilized by the large food service organization buyers, since the development of the formula itself and the attendant negotiation over what factors will be included in it are usually a time-consuming process. However, the development of such pricing formulas can be extremely beneficial to the large buyer who wants to maintain a close relationship between the price he is paying and the current market value for that product.

THE OPPORTUNITY BUY

Another approach which a large restaurant operation should consider is an opportunity buy. An opportunity buy may be defined as action taken by a buyer to take advantage of an unusual price situation which he realizes will only exist for a short period of time. During the course of any year, many such opportunities will present themselves to the buyer of a large chain operation. They may result from sudden over-supplies of a given item, as in the case of an unexpected decline in shrimp prices as a result of a bumper harvest in the Gulf of Mexico, or from an excess inventory being offered by the manufacturer at greatly reduced prices, as in the case of a manufacturer who is discontinuing an item and wishes to move his remaining inventory quickly. When an opportunity of this type comes up, the buyer should take several steps to determine whether it is in his company's best interest to take advantage of such a purchase.

DETERMINING THE VALUE OF AN OPPORTUNITY BUY

The first step is to compare the quality of the product available with the quality of a usual purchase. If they are comparable, the buyer should then consider a second question: How does the price of this opportunity item compare with the usual price of that item when purchased according to normal procedures over the same period of time? If there is a price saving of 10% or more, then the buyer should consider the opportunity price advantageous.

After a consideration of quality and price, the buyer should evaluate the cost of the opportunity buy. This should include the interest charges which the restaurant loses as a result of having its money tied up in an opportunity buy item, rather than being invested in either other aspects of the business or in the short-term money markets. If the buyer can realize 10% a year on his firm's money as a result of investing it in other aspects of the business or in short-term securities, then he must figure that the cost of executing this opportunity buy will be 10% per year, or $\frac{1}{12}$ of that amount for each month that his funds are tied up in the opportunity buy item. He must also figure the storage charges which he will incur if he is purchasing a long-term supply of the item. Once these two expenses have been identified, they can then be calculated in as the cost of implementing the opportunity buy.

AN EXAMPLE

Let us now apply these evaluation steps to a hypothetical opportunity buy example. Consider the case of a steak house chain which has an annual requirement of tenderloins of one hundred thousand pounds. In the next twelve months the buyer expects to see the price of tenderloins range between $2.50 and $3.50 per pound. However, due to a combination of market factors (such as actually occurred during November/December, 1974), he can now purchase tenderloins for $1.80 per pound.

The buyer knows that his requirement for this product is constant on a twelve-month basis, and that if he averages his projected prices for the next twelve months, he will come up with an average procurement cost of $3.00 per pound. He also knows that the quality of the product currently available at $1.80 per pound is consistent with the specification for his requirements. From past experience, the buyer recognizes that if they are properly packaged and frozen, tenderloins will keep for well over twelve months. Aware of these points, he then proceeds to the price comparison.

First, he sees that there is a potential saving of $1.20 per pound on this buy ($3.00 projected cost vs. $1.80 present availability cost). Based on a total purchase quantity of 100,000 pounds of tenderloins, he is therefore looking at a gross potential saving of $120,000. However, he must consider the cost of interest and storage charges on the purchase.

Since the purchase of 100,000 pounds at $1.80 per pound will require a capital commitment of $180,000, this is the figure on which the interest charges should be calculated. Assuming an interest rate of 10% on money invested in other ways, we look at an interest expense or added cost of approximately $18,000 a year or $1,500 a month. Since he will be consuming the merchandise in approximately equal monthly quantities over a twelve-month period, he can calculate this interest by cutting the twelve-month period in half. (Detailed calculations are shown in Figure 8.) Thus, we have an interest expense on the transaction of $8,230.

The next consideration is the cost of storage, which is 2¢ per pound per month, or 24¢ per pound per year. Again, as in the case of the interest charges, the actual storage rates are calculated by cutting the twelve-month period in half. Thus, the storage charges should be calculated at the rate of 12¢ per pound. Based on 100,000 pounds of merchandise, this is an expense of approximately $12,000 per year.

Thus, the total cost of implementing the opportunity buy amounts to $19,200 per year and must be subtracted from the $120,000 gross saving. This leaves a net opportunity buy saving of $100,800 or $1.008 per pound. As a percentage of the anticipated price, which would have otherwise been paid, this is a saving of 33%. Another way to look at this transaction is to say that the cost of implementing the opportunity buy is 19.2¢ per pound. Thus, for the entire effort to succeed, the average price of the tenderloins for the year would have to exceed $1.992 per pound (the opportunity cost of $1.80 plus the expense of implementation of 19.2¢ per pound).

While this example may seem extreme to some, it is truly remarkable how often opportunity buy situations arise. One word of caution, however: There have been many times in my experience when a particular market price seemed unusually attractive as a potential opportunity buy, but when the market actually declined even further from that level. Once a buyer decides to commit on an opportunity buy, he must recognize that he is locking in that price for the duration of the contract, and that if further price weaknesses develop, he will not be able to take advantage of them.

Part of the overall opportunity buy analysis should also include an examination of the effect of this purchase on the company's cash flow and cash position, since an expenditure of this magnitude obviously affects these two very important financial barometers. Another factor to be considered is the burden that this type of inventory in storage will place on the firm's existing storage facilities or any outside facility that might have to be leased. This question is not one relating to the 2¢ per pound per month storage charge, but rather one relating to available space and the pressures that might be created on other products normally stored in this space. A factor that is often overlooked is the additional personal property tax liability which would be created in those states having such tax regulations. Since personal property taxes are normally assessed on average inventories, the addition of this material tends to increase the personal property tax base, and therefore, the tax liability. This amount should be calculated as an added expense of the opportunity buy. Be especially careful of any

Figure 8   Calculations for opportunity buy

Expected price range high: $3.50 per pound
Expected price range low: $2.50 per pound

Requirement of 100,000 lbs: At average expected cost of $3.00/lb. (determined by averaging the high and low): a total annual expenditure of $300,000.

Potential savings by buying at $1.80/lb. and storing product is $120,000 less storage and handling charge:
($3.00 − $1.80 = $1.20 x 100,000 lbs. = $120,000)

Interest charges at 10% per annum on $180,000 (investment required to purchase the meat) is $18,000.

Since the meat will be used in equal amounts over a 12-month period, we will be figuring interest expense by using the charts opposite.

Analysis of Monthly Investment and Interest Expense
Initial purchase: 100,000 lbs. at $1.80 per lb.

Month	Remaining Balance Lbs.	x	$$ Investment $1.80	x	Monthly Interest Cost .0083
1	91,667		$165,001		$1,370*
2	83,334		150,001		1,245
3	75,001		135,002		1,121
4	66,668		120,002		996
5	58,335		105,003		872
6	50,002		90,004		747
7	41,669		75,004		623
8	33,336		60,005		498
9	25,003		45,005		374
10	16,670		30,006		249
11	8,337		15,007		125
Total interest cost					$8,220

*Month one of the calculation excludes 1/12 of the merchandise purchased, since that would go directly into the operation for consumption. Thus the starting quantity on which interest and storage charges are calculated is actually 91,667 lbs., which is 11/12 of the quantity originally purchased.

Detailed Analysis of Storage Cost

Month	Amount in Storage Lbs.	x	Rate of Expense .02¢/lb.
1	91,667		$ 1,833
2	83,334		1,667
3	75,001		1,500
4	66,668		1,333
5	58,335		1,167
6	50,002		1,000
7	41,669		833
8	33,336		667
9	25,003		500
10	16,670		333
11	8,337		167
12	--		--
Total			$11,000

insurance costs and/or potential higher casualty loss exposure as a result of adding this merchandise to your inventory.

PROFIT PLAN PROTECTION

Another item that the buyer should consider before implementing such buys is the net price of the buy over a period of time, and what type of locked-in profit he can realize as a result of knowing that commodity cost. If the profit from the opportunity buy exceeds his profit plan for the particular period, he should try to take advantage of the opportunity buy as a means of profit protection or improvement.

TERMS FROM VARIOUS SUPPLIERS

The well-versed buyer will also make a general evaluation of the terms available to him from various suppliers. Normally, terms refer to the discount arrangements which the vendor offers for prompt payment. However, there are other terms of purchase that must also be taken into account. Among these are minimum order size, delivery arrangements, including the number of deliveries per week, delivery days (whether the supplier is willing to deliver on a weekend), arrangements for emergency deliveries, and vendor policies on return of surplus merchandise. While not commonly thought of as key elements of the buying function, each of these can have a direct impact on the net cost of the items being purchased and should therefore be considered as such.

Discount Arrangements

Since discount arrangements are the most commonly discussed terms in a purchase arrangement between buyer and seller, let us first consider them. Normal discount arrangements call for a cash discount of one or two percent if the customer makes his payment to the vendor within ten days. If he does not, the full amount of the invoice is due after thirty days. However, there are other more specialized arrangements; for example, net amount due thirty days after the end of the month in which the purchases are made. In this case, the purchaser is receiving the additional use of the product without paying for it until thirty to sixty days after the purchase, depending upon the particular day of the month on which he made the purchase. During periods of slow cash flow, terms of this type might be quite advantageous to the buyer.

Another factor which the buyer should consider in negotiating his discount terms is his company's record of paying its bills. If he knows from past experience that the company regularly pays its bills in less than fourteen days, he might attempt to negotiate an even better cash discount than the one or two percent normally offered. In fact, in these days of tight and expensive money, such promptness can be worth more than that to a supplier who wants to be sure that he gets his money promptly.

However, there is no point in a buyer's attempt to negotiate special terms of this type unless he is absolutely certain that his firm's payment practices will consistently take advantage of them. Conversely, if he knows from past experience that his company does not take advantage of the cash discount periods, it might be worth his while to go to the suppliers and volunteer to give up the cash discount in exchange for a lower net price. In this instance, he simply says to the supplier that he would rather have the net price as low as possible, and that in the interest of working with the supplier toward that goal, he is willing to forego any cash discount allowance.

There are many other ways for the creative use of cash discounts, and over the course of a year they can amount to a very significant sum of money. For example, the restaurant operation spending $100,000 a year on food and supplies on which 1%–10, net 30 terms are generally in effect can save in excess of $1,000 if such terms are fully utilized.

Delivery Considerations

Among the other terms which the buyer should be fully cognizant of in his negotiations with various suppliers are those relating to delivery arrangements. Many vendors have minimum order requirements to protect themselves against the continuing high cost of delivery. If such is the case, the buyer may be required to accumulate his orders until he has developed a sufficient volume to meet the minimum order requirements of his various vendors. If he feels these minimum requirements are unrealistic or in any way unworkable as far as his operation is concerned, he should try to sit down with the vendor and attempt to negotiate an arrangement that will satisfy everyone. At all times he should be prepared to approach the vendor and present his particular needs in a very forthright and businesslike fashion. Depending on the vendor's desire to maintain this particular account, he might very well be willing to make exceptions to his otherwise inflexible rules.

Also in the delivery area is the important question of how many times per week the vendor is willing to make a delivery. This is particularly important for a restaurant that either has limited storage facilities or relies heavily on fresh meats, baked goods, and produce. Proper delivery arrangements can be a major contributing factor to maintaining both high quality standards and minimum inventories. Since inventories are money, unnecessary inventories are a financial strain on a restaurant's operation. It is especially important, therefore, that the buyer insist on arangements with suppliers that do not create inventory problems for his operation.

Another important, but frequently overlooked, requirement in the delivery area is the time of delivery. Vendors should be instructed not to make deliveries during peak business hours. Deliveries that arrive during the busiest (12 noon to 2 PM) meal periods are generally not checked as thoroughly as those which arrive during the slack periods (9:00–11:00 AM and 2:00–4:00 PM). Improper attention to incoming shipments can result in the purchase of poor quality products, improperly marked cuts of meat, short weight meats and produce, and other shortages that cost the restaurant significant losses.

In all too many cases, vendors are permitted to make deliveries during the busiest part of the business day. Chances are that when this occurs, deliveries are placed into the store's inventory using the vendor's invoice as the inventory entry document, rather than using a receiving ticket carefully prepared by the restaurant personnel. In addition to running the risk of inaccurate counts on incoming merchandise, the restaurant may not catch concealed shortages or damages ever, or until it is too late to file proper claims with the vendor. One of the absolute rules that every restaurant operation regardless of size should follow is: no deliveries between 12:00 noon and 2:00 PM. Most vendors understand the necessity for this rule, and if they are reliable and reputable businessmen, they will abide by it.

Placing Orders

Another important term that the buyer should review with all his vendors is the procedure for placing orders. In the case of repetitive purchases from known vendors, the buyer should try to arrange to have the vendor call for the prospective order at a prearranged time and day each week. If more than one vendor has submitted bids on a particular item, essentially the same procedure can be used, with the exception that two calls are required from each vendor; the first to submit his bid for the particular period, and the second, to find out if he has been the successful bidder and, if so, to take the order.

By placing the burden of order communication on the vendor, the buyer will reduce his own work load, and hence, his own overhead expense. Most vendors will not object to this method of order communication, because they believe it gives them better control of their communications with their customers. In fact, most vendors set up an order desk where they can make contact with their customers on a regular basis.

Emergency Shipments

Although no one plans them, there are times when a buyer needs emergency shipments from various vendors. He should discuss this possibility with his vendors and achieve an understanding as to how they will be handled. Proper response by a vendor to an emergency order can be very important to the smooth operation of a restaurant facility. However, restaurants that tend to take advantage of a supplier's willingness to provide emergency service quickly find themselves in the place of a young boy who cried, "Wolf!" once too often.

The buyer should instruct his operating people to avoid placing emergency orders unless absolutely necessary. If a member of the operating team can jump in a car and make a quick trip to a local supermarket to get an item that is unexpectedly out-of-stock, it is usually preferable to asking a supplier to make a special trip from a greater distance at an inconvenient hour with a small quantity of that item. Good judgment on the part of the buyer and his operating team is probably the best guideline to follow in placing emergency orders. A good buyer will place such requests sparingly. However, if an emergency should arise, he will not hesitate to ask his suppliers for assistance.

EQUIPMENT: TO LEASE OR TO PURCHASE

Another area that every buyer faces from time to time is the question of leasing versus purchasing equipment. In many cases, the suppliers of equipment such as soap dispensers, beverage dispensers for the soda fountain and bar, dishwashing machines, music systems, or rodent and insect control systems will offer the customer the alternative of leasing rather than purchasing the equipment. The decision of whether to lease or purchase should be based on two fundamental evaluations: 1) the cost of each, and 2) the availability of capital. You might also want to consider 3) the type of service available under each option, and 4) the equipment's potential for obsolescence.

The cost of leasing versus the cost of purchasing is figured out by determining the monthly or quarterly fee for leasing the equipment on an annualized basis and comparing that figure with the cost of outright purchase divided by the number of years during which the particular piece of equipment is expected to function. Adjustments for both figures should be taken into account.

In considering leasing fees, for example, the availability of funds which would otherwise be tied up in an outright purchase and which can be invested in short-term securities or in a savings account to generate interest reduces the annualized cost. Similarly, the interest lost on the money used for an outright purchase should be added to the purchase expense. After all such adjustments have been made, a comparison of the two amounts on an annualized basis will indicate whether lease or purchase is preferable. Figure 9 demonstrates this situation more specifically.

The other important consideration in leasing vs. purchasing is the availability of capital dollars for outright purchase. In many cases, particularly when a restaurant operation is just getting started, there may be a shortage of capital dollars, and although the economics may favor outright purchase, the owner of the restaurant may have no choice but to begin with a lease. If this occurs, he should reexamine the purchase alternative as soon as his capital position improves sufficiently to allow him to do so.

The type of equipment service which is available under each option is also an important question. If the vendor is willing to provide service of equal caliber under either option, then you can discount this as a consideration. However, if there is any question at all regarding

**Analysis of a lease vs. purchase
of a double deck convection oven**

Purchase	
Cost if purchased	$1,700
Sales tax @ 5%	85
Shipping charges	35
Installation charge	50
Total cost	$1,870

Annual service contract after first year: $30/year

Lease

Cost of lease: $40/month
No sales tax.
Shipping, installation and service at no charge.
　　Lease cost per year: $480.00
　　　($40/month x 12 months)
　　Estimated useful life of equipment:
　　　7 years.
7 years at $480/year = $3,360 total cost of lease.

Thus if the operator expects to be in business for seven years or more, the outright purchase would be the least expensive alternative.

The breakeven point (the point in time when lease payments equal the purchase price) is three years and 11 months. (This is figured by dividing the monthly lease fee of $40 into the purchase (price: $1,870÷$40 = 46.75 months.)

Other considerations:

Benefit of purchasing: The trade-in value of the equipment is a credit against the purchase price.

Benefit of leasing: Avoiding the danger of equipment obsolescence prior to the expiration of its seven-year useful life.

Figure 9

the supplier's reliability in servicing equipment which is purchased outright, then the buyer might be better off leasing it (all other things are equal, of course).

A final consideration in the lease/purchase decision is the potential for obsolescence of the particular piece of equipment during its lifetime. For example, if you expect a particular type of music system to be obsolete within a few years, there is very little point in an outright purchase when a new and improved system might come on the market long before the purchaser has gotten his full money's worth from it. The best way for a buyer to determine this question is to carefully study the particular piece of equipment and to talk to a sufficient number of suppliers to get a pretty good idea of the chance for obsolescence before the useful life of the equipment has expired.

Chapter 4 Questions

1. Discuss the law of supply and demand as it relates to food prices.

2. How does the timing of purchases influence the price to be paid for a particular item?

3. Discuss the pros and cons of market price date of shipment versus fixed price purchase long-term purchase contracts.

4. How can the buyer utilize variations in purchase terms to improve the quality of his purchase?

5. What factors should the buyer keep in mind in scheduling deliveries of merchandise?

6. What factors should the buyer consider when deciding whether to lease a piece of equipment or purchase it outright?

5

Buying Strategy

WHAT IS A BUYING STRATEGY?

As the purchasing profession becomes more sophisticated, there is more discussion of a firm's buying strategy. This is nothing more than the game plan that a particular organization intends to use in covering their requirements for goods and services. It evolves from the general operating philosophy of the restaurant and concentrates specifically on the various procurement problems which it faces. It includes such considerations as the quality of the food to be served, the type of customer desired, and the profit margin goals that have been established. These goals are then used as an umbrella for the development of specific purchasing guidelines. Simply stated, then, the buying strategy is a statement of how the organization plans to take care of its purchasing requirements in order to attain the overall operating goals which it has set for itself.

SOME EXAMPLES

A general buying strategy, for example, might state that, "We intend to use local suppliers wherever product quality and price are consistently competitive in order to strengthen the image of our restaurant as a local operation." Or, for a different type restaurant, the buying strategy might be, "We intend to purchase frozen, precooked items wherever possible in order to enhance our overall goal of maintaining the least possible labor cost." Again emanating directly from the operating philosophy of the particular operation, still another strategy might be, "Wherever available, we intend to purchase strictly fresh fruits and produce and fresh poultry and seafood on a seasonably available basis in order to support our image as a high quality restaurant with a menu that changes according to the seasons."

To illustrate the diversity of these buying strategies in various restaurant operations, let us look at a few that have been formulated from different points of view. One restaurant chain bases its operations on a buying strategy that says, "Whenever the price of our top fifty most important raw materials reaches a level equal to or below the price which has been included in our profit forecast for the next monthly, quarterly, or annual period, we will purchase our requirements so that we can fix the price at a level equal to or below the approved profit plan." More simply stated, that strategy means that if the firm can purchase its raw materials at prices which allow the firm to sell the product at margins consistent with its approved profit plan, then it will do so in order to lock in these margins. Actually, this is a very conservative and sound buying strategy for a large chain.

Another approach that might be used in any size restaurant operation is a buying strategy which states, "All procurement will be based on a fifty/fifty combination of fixed price, long-term contracts and purchases made on the current market." This buying strategy is essentially one of hedging your purchase: half the requirements use fixed price purchasing based on the buyer's judgment of future price activity and the other fifty percent are purchased at the current market price. Few financial planners would find fault with such a strategy, since it attempts to combine the best features of fixed price contracts, which are based on the buyer's judgment of future price trends, and current market buying, which offers the security of averaging those purchases. This is where the hedge comes in. The fifty percent of requirements that is purchased on the fixed price contract is "hedged" by keeping the other fifty percent open to be bought at prevailing market prices at the time of actual need.

It is important that every restaurant organization, from the individual operation up to the largest chain, carefully determine its own particular buying strategy and commit this strategy to paper.

This way, there will be no doubt in the minds of those implementing the strategy as to what the final goals are.

IMPLEMENTING YOUR BUYING STRATEGY

Once you have clearly defined the buying strategy, you can develop plans for implementing this strategy. This is done through a buying plan. Whereas the buying strategy is usually in a conceptual form, the buying plan converts this concept into reality.

The buying plan involves specific steps that the buyer must take to implement the buying strategy. It may be as simple as three or four statements on a piece of paper detailing the specific suppliers which the restaurant plans to use as its vendors, along with a brief description of order quantities, target inventory levels, and specific purchasing procedures it will aim for. On the other hand, it might be a fairly detailed document that specifies the sources of supply, order patterns, delivery schedules, pricing and billing requirements, specifications, etc., for each specific commodity group (meat, seafood, poultry, produce, etc.).

The degree of detail in the buying plan really depends on the needs of a particular operation. However, there is one important point to keep in mind: The more accurately a buying plan reflects the company's buying strategy, the more likely it is that the restaurant will carry out its purchasing activities on a basis that is compatible with the overall operating goals of the establishment. The old truism, "Plan your work and then work your plan" is particularly apt in the development and use of a buying plan that is tailored to the needs of the particular restaurant or chain.

CONSIDERATIONS IN ESTABLISHING A BUYING STRATEGY

In the consideration of buying strategies, a buyer should purchase on the basis of both long-term, fixed price commitment and on the current market price. Essentially all types of specific purchasing activity fall into these two categories. Since both approaches have their own very firm and avid supporters, let's take a moment to consider the pros and cons of each approach as they will apply to both the individual operation and the chain.

The Long-Term, Fixed Price Method of Purchasing

The long-term, fixed price method of procurement is very, very good when the buyer's judgment regarding price activity or available supply is accurate. However, when his judgment is poor (and all of us, no matter how extensive our training, have occasionally been wrong), then this type of contract can be very, very bad.

There are many "horror stories" in the restaurant industry of buyers who purchase and take delivery of a large quantity of an item a week or so before it is declared illegal, immoral, obsolete, or its value drops by fifty percent. There is the story of the buyer for a large restaurant chain who purchased and took delivery of 100,000 pounds of swordfish two weeks before the famous mercury scare broke in the press several years ago. Although there was nothing wrong with the fish this buyer had bought (extensive laboratory tests confirmed this fact), customers were so concerned by what they had read and heard that they would order none of the swordfish items on the menu.

Perhaps more frequent than a scare of this type is the situation in which a buyer executes a long-term contract on a particular item he feels is attractively priced and will become more expensive, only to see a sharp break in the price even before the ink is dry on the purchase order.

Naturally, the converse of this situation can happen for the buyer who watches the market closely and defers his purchase commitments in anticipation of further price weakness. How many restaurant buyers, for example, were caught unprepared for the sudden rise in sugar prices which began during the late spring of 1974 and continued uninterrupted throughout the remainder of the year?

Thus, we can see that long-term, fixed price purchase commitments can be both a blessing and a curse. It is somewhat like a scapel in the hands of a skilled surgeon. When the scapel is sharp, the surgeon is able to accomplish great results with it. However, if it is dull, the results can be disastrous. As a general rule, the larger the restaurant operation, the more carefully it should monitor long-term, fixed price purchase contracts. This is so for a number of reasons:

- Since a larger operation has greater raw material requirements, it can develop significant purchasing leverage in negotiating the most advantageous long-term, fixed price contract possible.

- The larger the organization and the greater its financial resources, the more able it will be to enter into this type of contract in a manner that will satisfy the vendor that the vendor will receive performance from the buyer. These resources also protect the buyer in the event that the purchase turns out to be disadvantageous.
- Theoretically, the buying personnel of the large organization have sufficient expertise in the purchase of a particular commodity so that they have a fairly good "feel" for its price movements. If this is in fact the case, these buying personnel should be more astute judges of the proper timing in establishing these long-term commitments than the buyer for the individual restaurant or small chain would be.

This is certainly not to suggest that the savvy buyer for the small operation will not have every bit as much technique and purchasing skill as the buyer for the larger operation. In my personal experience, some of the most perceptive commodity buyers I have ever encountered have been the owners and operators of individual restaurants who have followed a particular item or group of items closely for a number of years and are remarkably talented in forecasting both the short- and long-term price movements of these items. As with everything else in life, good market judgment is a matter of practice and experience. But even liberal doses of both cannot guarantee that the buyer will always be correct.

Any restaurant organization that sees an advantage in using the long-term, fixed price commitments should start preparing for the adoption of this technique well in advance of its implementation. This preparation process should include information relating to past market price performance for at least a two-year period on the items they are interested in buying. If information is available for a period longer than that, it should be noted.

Studying this price information will give the buyer some initial guidelines as to the month-to-month and year-to-year price fluctuations for the item. Buyers are frequently quite surprised to see how obvious these price patterns become once they are laid out over an extended period of time. (See Figure 10).

Next, the buyer should contact several purveyors who handle this type of product and attempt to glean as much information as possible from them as to the cycles, movements, supply/demand characteristics

Figure 10   CHOICE STEER PRICES FOB OMAHA

900-1100 lbs. weight.
Average price by quarter.

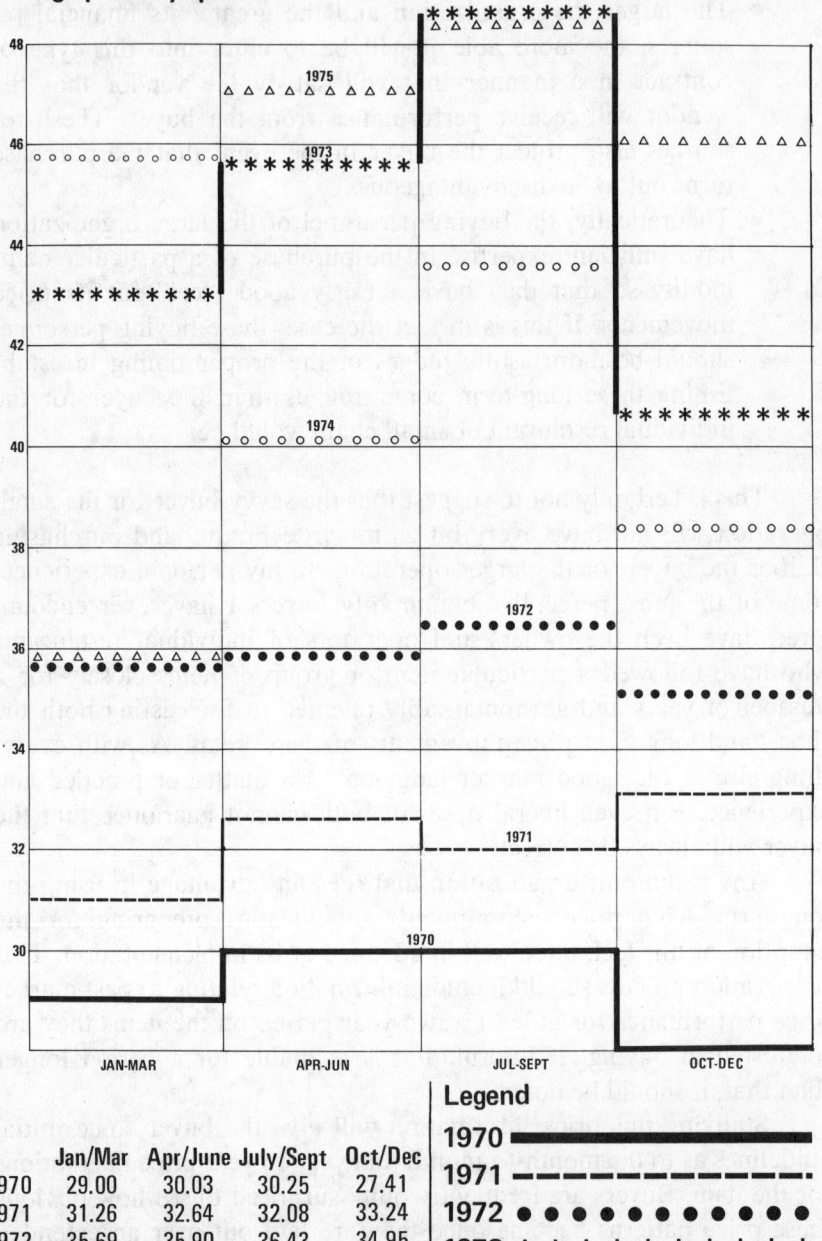

	Jan/Mar	Apr/June	July/Sept	Oct/Dec
1970	29.00	30.03	30.25	27.41
1971	31.26	32.64	32.08	33.24
1972	35.69	35.90	36.43	34.95
1973	42.96	45.73	49.75	40.70
1974	45.37	40.20	43.70	38.30
1975	35.76	47.22	48.64	46.00

Legend
1970 ——————
1971 – – – – – –
1972 ● ● ● ● ● ● ● ●
1973 * * * * * * * *
1974 ○ ○ ○ ○ ○ ○ ○ ○
1975 △ △ △ △ △ △ △ △

At first glance the symbols scattered across this chart may appear to be nothing more than a random scattering of price movements. However, the chart tells a very interesting story. During the six-year period from 1970 through 1975, in four of the six years, the lowest average price for choice steers on an Omaha market basis occurred during the months of October to December. Only in 1971 and 1975 did the lowest price occur in another calendar quarter, and in both cases these lows occurred during the first calendar quarter of those years. In 1971 we can theorize that the first quarter low was a carryover resulting from continued supply pressure on prices during the fourth quarter of 1970. In 1975 the same situation developed as a result of supply pressure on prices during the fourth quarter of 1974. This is an excellent example of seasonal price patterns.

The buyer who watches price movements like this can identify patterns in movement that will help guide him in the timing of his purchases. Obviously, in the case of choice steers (which serve as the price basis on which choice cuts of meat-ribs-loins-strips, etc., are costed), the ideal time to purchase is during the fourth quarter of each calendar year, while the second best time to buy is during the first quarter of the calendar year. By having such information in hand, the buyer is in a much better position to plan and time his procurement activities.

Unfortunately, the year-to-year trend of price increases results in a condition where prices in 1975 were 40%-50% higher than in 1970.

of the product and resultant price reactions. Since such suppliers have probably been handling this product for many years, they are about as familiar with its price characteristics as anyone could be. As a part of their sales development activities, they will usually be willing to share this knowledge with an interested buyer.

Another excellent source of price and supply information is another user of the same item or items. Discussions with other users at association meetings, trade shows, conferences, and the like will frequently turn up very interesting perspectives from others who are faced with the same type of procurement problems. The buyer should recognize that it is no disgrace to ask questions. In fact, people who are asked questions are usually quite flattered that their opinion is of high regard and will therefore be delighted to share it quite freely.

After this information gathering process has been completed, the buyer is essentially on his own to evaluate the information and make his market judgments. Rather than taking this new-found information and plunging into the market, the buyer would be much wiser to consummate, on paper only, a number of hypothetical, long-term, fixed price purchase commitments wherein he selects the quantity of product he wishes to purchase and the date on which he feels the price is most advantageous. He should then track his hypothetical purchase commitment over the period of time it would take to exhaust the supply he had hypothetically purchased.

By tracking the actual market price performance during this period against his hypothetical contract, he will be in a position to evaluate the efficacy of his hypothetical actions. (See Figure 11.) If he has been successful in a number of such hypothetical actions, he would then be ready to begin experimenting with the real thing. However, the initial stages of actual purchase should be done in very small quantities and for relatively limited periods of time. Since long-term, fixed price purchase commitments can have such a significant effect on the profitability or loss of a restaurant operation, they should not be undertaken without very careful evaluation and a gradual build-up in the quantity of the material purchased.

Purchasing on the Basis of Current Market Value

On the other side of the purchasing alternative is the school of buyers who say, "As long as we buy on the current market, we never have to worry about paying too much for our product." To that line of reasoning, I might also add, "nor will they ever pay less than the current market."

There are very definite times when this philosophy of procurement makes excellent business sense for the restaurant industry. The most obvious is during a time when in the buyer's judgment market prices are entering a weakening cycle. Certainly, if the buyer expects prices to move lower over a period of weeks or months, it would not be to his advantage to consummate a long-term, fixed price purchase, unless his suppliers shared his anticipation of weaker prices and were willing to discount the price quotation to reflect this expected downward movement. Another time when a buyer might justify restricting his actions to current market price procurement would be in anticipation of removing a particular item from the menu. In this case, the buyer is following a minimum inventory policy. This approach certainly makes sense if there is a reasonable expectation that the item will not be required in the future.

However, other than within these two conditions, a firm's continuing use of near-term market price buying as its primary purchasing tool will produce poorer results for a restaurant operation. I can certainly understand using it in combination with long-term, fixed price purchase commitments as a partial hedge against an adverse price move on items under long-term contract. But short of that situation it is not a viable, ongoing purchasing technique.

COMMODITY FUTURES MARKETS

Any discussion of food purchasing for the restaurant industry, especially for the larger chain operations, eventually gets around to the subject of commodity futures. The use of the commodity futures markets is very possibly the least understood commercial technique in the business world. Most people who are vaguely familiar with the existence of commodity futures markets place them in the same category as the two-dollar bet at the race track or the weekly purchase of a lottery ticket.

In fact, this could not be further from the truth. For many commodities, the commodity futures market, when properly used for purely hedging purposes, provides the only means available to the user to obtain protection against adverse price movement. This protection is obtained by a very straight-forward device known as *hedging*.

Figure 11   BONELESS STRIP LOINS

market price/pound over a one-year period

——————— AVERAGE MONTHLY CASH PRICE—LOCAL MARKET

– – – – – – – COVERAGE PRICE CONTRACTED BY BUYER

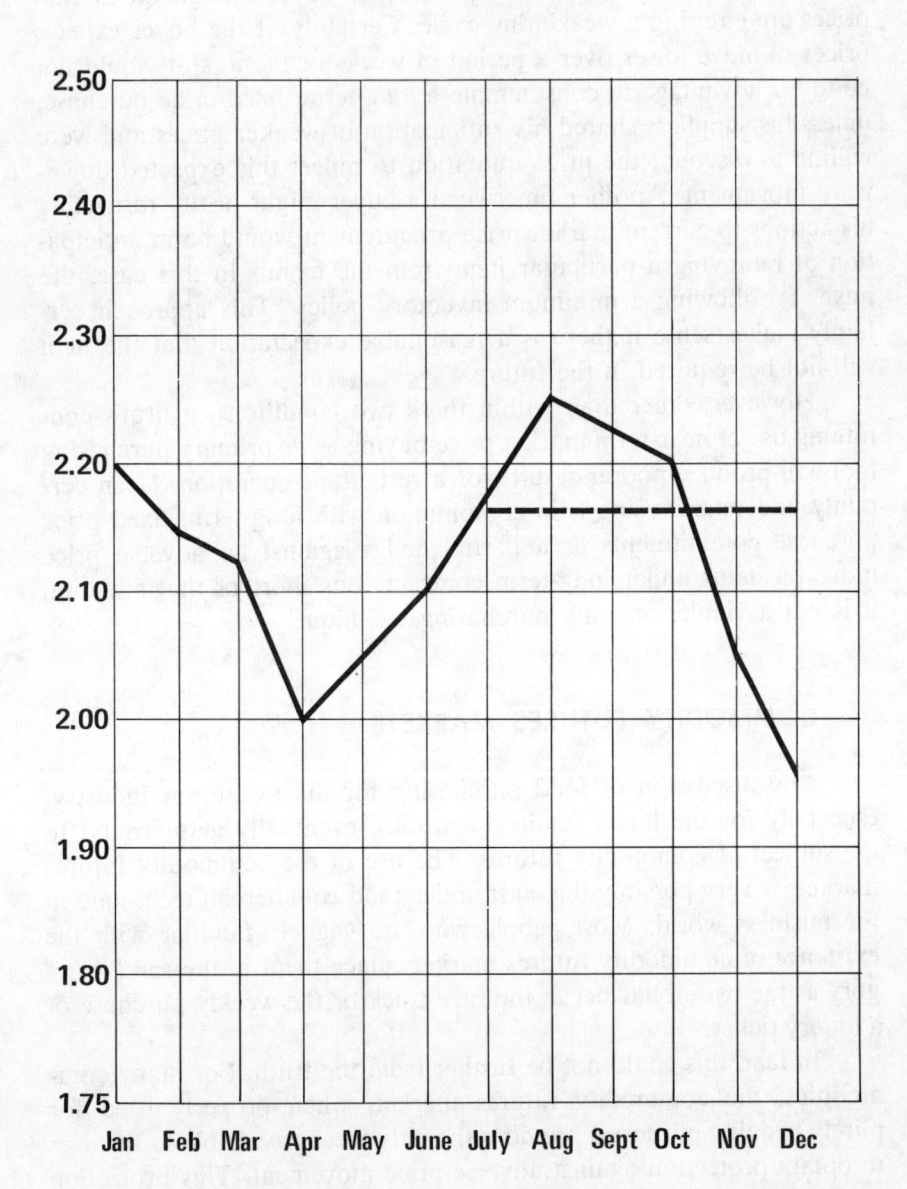

In this particular illustration, the buyer followed the cash market for boneless strip loins through the first six months of the year and decided at that point that he had sufficient market judgment to warrant implementing a hypothetical coverage level for the second half of the year at a fixed price of $2.18 per pound. The cash market price movements during that period show us a very interesting pattern, although the buyer obviously had no way of knowing it at the time he implemented the coverage.

First, he was right in his market judgment that prices were going to advance. But he was wrong on two very important counts: 1) He waited too long to implement the coverage which ideally should have been made during the April/May period when the price was down close to $2.00 per pound. And 2) he then extended the coverage for too long so that the cash market price was substantially below his coverage level by the time the coverage expired. Rather than implementing the coverage for a period of six months, he would have been far better to have implemented it only through the month of October, thereby taking advantage of a 25¢ per pound break in price between October 1st and December 31st.

Thus, in this particular example, we see that the buyer was essentially right in his initial market judgment, but wrong on two counts that far outweighed the correctness of his coverage decision. Any person who intends to participate in food procurement should put himself through a similar set of exercises to test his own market judgment prior to actually entering into raw material coverage situation. Regular exposure to this type of tracking of one's market judgment will quickly enable a buyer to get a reading on his own abilities in this area.

Hedging simply means trying to avoid or offset possible loss in purchasing a commodity by making an opposite, counterbalancing investment in the futures market for that commodity.

Consider the case of the fast food chain which features fried chicken as its primary menu offering. The raw material used to produce breaded fried chicken is iced broilers. The price of iced broilers fluctuates over a range of from 7 to 10 cents per pound during a normal supply year and can range as much as 10 to 15 cents per pound during a year when supplies are interrupted, or when feed prices show sharp movements. For a product whose average price is in the low 40 cents per pound range, this is a very significant range of price variation.

Since iced broilers cannot be kept for more than a few days, most restaurants that use them for fried chicken have no alternative but to buy their requirements on a regular weekly basis. An exception to this is the operation that buys the raw chicken at a time when the price seems attractive and then stores the finished breaded product in the frozen state until the time of consumption. While such action may be advantageous for many companies, it is not without its own risk factors, since the market price may not go up as anticipated by the buyer or, even worse, may decline, resulting in an inventory loss. In addition, storing large quantities of finished product in the frozen state can be an expensive alternative.

The use of the iced broiler futures market (this commodity is traded on the Chicago Board of Trade) provides a hedging opportunity for any operation consuming substantial quantities of breaded fried chicken. In order to utilize the futures market, the restaurant operator need not be a primary producer of the breaded fried chicken, as are some of the major restaurant chains in their own manufacturing facilities. He might very well be purchasing the product either frozen prebreaded from a local grocery distributor, or on a raw basis for on-site breading at his individual location.

In order to apply the principles of hedging in this situation, the operator would identify his anticipated consumption of breaded fried chicken on a monthly basis for a specific period of time. He would then purchase an equal quantity of iced broiler futures to be delivered during several months spaced across the period of time on which his consumption forecast is developed.

It is not necessary that he buy the actual cash broilers at this time, since they will be purchased on an as-needed basis later on.

ICED BROILER BUYING HEDGE
ESTABLISHED ON 3/15
WHEN CASH WAS 39¢ LB. & FUTURES 41¢ LB.

	Cash	Futures	Profit (Loss) On purchase of cash	Profit (Loss) On sale of futures contract
April	39¢	41¢	– 0 –	– 0 –
May	41¢	43¢	(2)	2
June	42¢	44¢	(3)	3
July	46¢	48¢	(7)	7
August	47¢	49¢	(8)	8
September	45¢	47¢	(6)	6

Note: The difference between the cash and the futures prices is called the basis. In this example it is 2¢ per pound.

As the futures coverage for each month is sold off and cash product is purchased, the profit on the futures is used to offset the loss (higher purchase price compared to price on 3/15) of the cash product.

Figure 12

Similarly, it is not necessary that he take delivery of these futures contracts when delivery comes due, because they will be sold off (liquidated) as the cash product is purchased to fill operating needs. The act of selling off the futures at a later date removes the hedge (price protection) which he established when he purchased the futures.

For purposes of this example, let's assume that his monthly consumption is 36,000 pounds, which happens to equal the quantity of iced broilers covered by one futures contract on the Chicago Board of Trade. Assuming he is covering his requirements for a six month period (April thru September), since he expects broiler prices to increase, he would purchase six contracts of iced broiler futures. Figure 12 summarizes the pertinent figures on both sides of this transaction, showing not only the price movement in both the cash and futures market during the six month period, but also the impact of the hedging transaction on both the cash and futures sides of the hedge.

An analysis of this transaction shows that although the cash price of broilers increased throughout the period covered by the hedging transaction, the profit made in liquidating (selling off) the futures which had previously been purchased at the time the hedge was established can be applied against the higher cost of the cash broilers, thereby bringing the cash broiler price back to the 39¢ per pound figure, which applied on March 15th when the hedge was originally established. This is the essence of hedging: protection; an insurance policy; to guard against adverse price movements which have a negative impact on profit margins. The profit realized on the futures side of the transaction is not looked upon by the hedger as a profit. Rather, it is considered to be an offset against the higher cash price which he was required to pay as the general market for iced broilers advanced.

Of course, the hedge could have turned out to be unprofitable on the futures side, if for some unexpected reason cash and futures prices had declined during the six month period of the hedge. Since there is always the chance that this type of price action will occur, let us consider for a moment the consequences on the firm's actual price of cash broilers.

Figure 13 demonstrates this situation, wherein cash and futures prices moved lower during the period covered by the hedging transaction. In this case we see that although a loss was incurred on the futures side of the transaction, the buyer was able to purchase his cash requirements for iced broilers at prices correspondingly below the price which existed at the time the hedge was established. Hence, he can consider the savings realized by his purchase of cash iced broilers at a lower price than originally anticipated as an offset against the loss of the futures side of the transaction. Obviously, in this case the buyer would have been better off had he not instituted the hedging transaction, but as a wise man once said, "Hindsight is always 20/20."

The key point to remember when considering a hedging transaction as a purchasing tool is that it is a protective device designed to guard against the erosion of known profit margins. At no time should it be considered as a potential profit-making opportunity. Further-

ICED BROILER BUYING HEDGE ESTABLISHED ON 3/15 WHEN CASH WAS 39¢ LB. AND FUTURES 41¢ LB.

	Cash	Futures	Profit (Loss) On purchase of cash	Profit (Loss) On sale of futures
April	39¢	41¢	– 0 –	– 0 –
May	38¢	40¢	1	(1)
June	36¢	38¢	3	(3)
July	35¢	37¢	4	(4)
August	35¢	37¢	4	(4)
September	34¢	36¢	5	(5)

Note that in each case the loss on the futures is offset by the lower purchase price of the cash in the same month compared to the price at the time the hedge was initiated.

Figure 13

more, hedging is a very sophisticated procurement technique and should not be attempted unless qualified commodity experts are handling the transaction.

Another example of the use of hedging would be the case of a large restaurant chain that consumes one million pounds of shortening per year in its various frying operations. They expect shortening prices to move upward over the next twelve months but are unable to get price commitments from their shortening suppliers for more than two weeks at a time. To protect themselves against what they fear will be an upward price move, they establish what is known as a *buying hedge*.

In this situation they purchase sufficient futures contracts of soy bean oil (the major ingredient in most shortenings used for deep frying) to equal the amount of shortening they anticipate using during the year. In this case the futures purchase represents the long side (what they own) of the hedge, while their actual need for the product (against which the futures will be applied) represents the short side (what they will need) of the hedging transaction.

If, in fact, their market judgment is correct and shortening prices do advance, they will be required to pay higher prices for their actual shortening as they purchase it in the future. But they will sell the futures contracts, which will also have increased in price at a profit. The profit on the futures contracts will then be used to offset the higher cost of the actual shortening, thus returning the shortening price to the point where it was at the time the initial hedging transaction was initiated.

Conversely, if for some reason the shortening market declined after the hedge was established, the firm would be able to purchase its shortening requirements at a lower price than originally anticipated (thus saving themselves money against their planned cost), and at the same time would have a loss on the future contracts, which they would be simultaneously selling. The loss on the futures would be offset by the savings (profit) on the cash product which they were able to purchase at a lower price. Thus again we see the offsetting nature of the hedging transaction.

The foregoing examples may seem confusing to the reader seeking an in-depth understanding of the commodity futures market and hedging transactions. While I have tried to give the reader a basic understanding of these two areas, any reader who desires further information on the commodity futures markets should contact one of the major brokerage houses. There are also a number of excellent books that have been written on the subject.

Commodity futures as a hedging device can be extremely helpful to the restaurant firm that has properly trained people who understand the commodity markets and can work with brokers in executing hedging transactions. A word of caution, however, is in order. At no time should any restaurant operator attempt to utilize the commodity futures markets unless he thoroughly understands their operation and is establishing a hedging transaction. Under no circumstances can speculation in the commodity futures market be justified as a legitimate business transaction. Speculation is for the speculators and restaurant operators, although they have been called many things, cannot qualify as commodity speculators.

The commodity futures markets offer another tool to the buyer, regardless of the size of the operation for which he is buying. Since

Products Commonly Used in a Food Service Operation for Which There Exists a Commodity Futures Market

ITEM	COMMODITY FUTURES
Bacon	Pork bellies
Broilers	Iced broilers
Orange concentrate	Orange concentrate
Potatoes	Maine potatoes
	Idaho potatoes
Beef items	Cattle*
Pork items	Hogs*
Sugar	Sugar
Cocoa	Cocoa
Soy bean oil	Soy bean oil
Eggs	Shell eggs
Coffee	Coffee

*Use of these futures is considered to be an imperfect hedge, since the commodity traded on the futures market is not exactly the same as the cash item being hedged. For example, a rib of beef will have a different price movement than a whole steer. However, the price of the two items (the rib of beef and the steer) will generally tend to move in the same direction; hence, a partial hedging opportunity is still present.

Figure 14

the commodity futures market deals in products for future delivery, they can be considered an excellent barometer of price activity expected in the future. An astute buyer should make it a practice to look at the commodity futures prices on a daily basis for all those items which he purchases for his restaurant operation. In short order, he will recognize a distinct relationship between the price of the commodity futures and the actual cash item. By recognizing this relationship and acting accordingly in his actual cash purchases, the buyer will very often be able to anticipate price changes in the cash market before they are apparent to his competition, or, in some cases, to his suppliers. Figure 14 lists those items commonly used in restaurant operations for which there is presently commodity futures trading. It is interesting to note the wide variety of commodity futures which are available for the legitimate hedging operation.

TIMING

It has often been said that the biggest individual factor in a person's success in the business world is being in the right place at the right time. Timing is generally considered to be an essential ingredient in the effectiveness of almost every human endeavor. Nowhere is this generalization more accurate than in the effective execution of a food service company's purchasing activities.

The difference between a good and a bad buy on several key ingredients can readily spell the difference between profit and loss in many limited menu food service operations. During the chicken crisis of late 1973, a number of profitable fast food companies slipped into red ink. Because their menu emphasized chicken, they had no way to control the sudden upward move in the price of chicken while menu price controls were in operation. The more broadly based food service companies could avoid this problem by simply downplaying chicken on their menus during this period.

Developing a sense of market timing is critically important for any buyer in the food service industry. This sense of timing is not an inherent sense found in the vast majority of food service buyers. But it is a technique that is developed after careful and painstaking experience with various commodities and their price/supply cycles.

A buyer should practice his timing techniques for a period of time before actually putting them into practice. This practice is usually best carried out by taking "paper positions" in various products. For example, a food service buyer might decide to make a number of theoretical purchases in the egg market at different times of the year when he feels prices are about to increase. He could then track the results of his "paper purchase" during the period of time in which the merchandise would theoretically be consumed. By tracking the price at which he had effected his "paper coverage" and by comparing it to actual prices during the period, he would then be able to evaluate how well his theoretical purchase would have done as compared with the actual marketplace.

Naturally, in a time when the buyer expected egg prices to decline, he would buy on what is commonly called a "hand-to-mouth" basis. This simply means that the buyer buys no more than he needs for immediate consumption on a daily or weekly basis in anticipation of lower prices the next time he enters the marketplace. This whole approach to theoretical buying is essential in training the buyer for the food service operation.

Chapter 5 Questions

1. How would you define a food service firm's buying strategy?

2. What is the difference between a firm's buying strategy and its buying plan?

3. What are the pros and cons of the long-term, fixed price contract method of procurement?

4. What are the advantages and disadvantages of short-term, market price date-of-shipment buying programs?

5. How can a food service operation utilize the commodity futures market as a procurement device?

6

Food Buying

GIVE COMPLETE SPECIFICATIONS

Before a buyer for a restaurant or for a contract feeder can even begin to think about the actual buying activity, he must have complete specifications for whatever he plans to purchase. In many buying situations the lack or incompleteness of specifications not only creates major problems for the food service organization, but also creates difficulties for the supplier who conscientiously attempts to deliver exactly what the buyer wants. Naturally, there are other less conscientious purveyors who will greet the absence of specifications with great enthusiasm, since this condition gives them a carte blanche to deliver whatever grade of merchandise they choose. In the case of the small dollar purchase, a shipment which is unacceptable because of incomplete specifications can usually be adjudicated with a reliable supplier or avoided entirely in the future by terminating the business relationship with an unreliable supplier. However, if the case involves a major dollar purchase such as a large chain or contract feeder might enter into, a breakdown in the specifications can have disastrous results.

One of my associates with a medium-sized seafood chain had an opportunity several years ago to purchase a large quantity of scallops which were a key item on his firm's menu. Since he would not be using the scallops for some months to come, his contract called for the scallops to be put in storage for his account. After giving his specifications to the supplier and inspecting a sample, he entered into a contract for 50,000 pounds of product at $2.50 per pound.

Much to his surprise, when he withdrew the first shipment from storage some months later, he found that he had purchased 50,000 pounds of sea scallops (25 to the pound), when in fact the sample he had seen and the quantity he had thought he was purchasing were bay scallops (90 to 120 to the pound). When he contacted the supplier to complain about the product, the supplier very quickly pointed out that the specification which had become a part of the purchase order did not specify the count of scallops to the pound and that the buyer therefore had no grounds for rejection.

The buyer immediately concluded that he was being "ripped off" by an unscrupulous purveyor and took steps through a trade association to have the matter resolved. It was only after a substantial delay, an expenditure of several thousand dollars in attorney's fees and travel expenses, and considerable disruption to his own firm's supply of scallops, to say nothing of the higher price which he subsequently had to pay to replace the product, that the buyer resolved the matter. Needless to say, this experience has taught him the importance of having complete and accurate specifications for every product.

The specifications should state in clear and simple terms the name of the product to be purchased and all its pertinent characteristics. This may include its size, shape, weight, color, texture, moisture content, density, smell, fat content (in the case of meat products), etc. Frequently, the size is described by what is called a *count,* as in the case of hamburgers (either four to the pound or six to the pound) and dill pickle spears (90 to 100 to a number 10 can).

In addition to the product description, you should give a complete and accurate description of the way the product is to be packaged. This is particularly important if the product is being purchased on a F.O.B. basis (the supplier's liability ceases at the time the product leaves his location), or if the product is to be stored either in transit or at the consumer's location. During my eighteen years in the food business, I have seen literally hundreds of thousands of dollars worth of food products either damaged or lost entirely as a result of faulty packaging. Although packaging costs are constantly on the rise, there is still no excuse for skimping on adequate packaging. No matter how expensive the packaging becomes, the product within is usually more expensive and thus costly to lose, especially for a reason as poor as faulty packaging.

Figures 15, 16, and 17 illustrate typical examples of food specifications that are currently used in the food service industry. As a general rule, it is best to keep the specifications as simple as possible in providing complete information to the purveyor as to the product being purchased. If the specifications are complete, then any disputes over the merchandise delivered can generally be adjudicated with little controversy. To whatever degree these specifications are incomplete, the buyer loses control over the quality of the products shipped to him. Thus a proper quality control function cannot operate unless the specifications which the firm has established are complete.

DETAIL PROCEDURES TO BE USED

In addition to the characteristics of the product being purchased, good specifications should also detail the procedures that will be used by the receiving and quality control representatives to test and evaluate the merchandise that is received.

If, for example, a restaurant intends to test the fat content of the hamburger it receives, the specification should also detail the particular fat testing method which the firm will use. Because there are a number of different fat testing methods presently in use, different methods can produce different results. If the food service operation is using one method and the purveyor, another, they can end up with significantly different results which could easily lead to an unresolvable dispute.

In addition, for any product packed in water, it is extremely important that the draining procedures and times be carefully explained in the specification. This avoids disputes with the purveyor regarding the drained weight of the merchandise received. When draining procedures are not followed, the consuming restaurant always runs the risk of buying water or some other liquid in lieu of the particular item it thought it was purchasing.

Thus, specifications will not guarantee the absence of any problems with purveyors, but they certainly can go a long way toward eliminating many of the disputes that relate to product quality.

MATERIAL SPECIFICATION

1. **ITEM:**
   Squash

2. **DESCRIPTION:**
   A canned product prepared from clean, sound, properly matured, golden fleshed, sweet varieties of squashes by washing, stemming, cutting, steaming and reducing to pulp.

3. **PACKAGING:**
   Product to be packed in a #10 tin can which in turn are packed six to the corrugated case. Corrugated case must have a minimum bursting strength of 250 lbs.

4. **SPECIAL LABELING REQUIREMENTS:**
   The product label must be clear and legible and conform to all local, state and federal regulations.

5. **CHEMICAL/BACTERIAL REQUIREMENTS:**

6. **SPECIAL INSTRUCTIONS/REQUIREMENTS:**
   U.S. Grade A or U.S. Fancy product is properly sieved during processing and sufficiently heat treated to insure preservation in hermetically sealed cans. The color should be uniform and bright and characteristic of mature processed squash. The consistency of the product should be firm enough to hold the shape of the container or remain in a mound when emptied from the can. The product should be free from extraneous matter, seeds, and dark or off colored particles.

Figure 15

By handing this specification to a prospective supplier, the buyer is communicating exactly what his needs are for this particular product. The supplier can then review this specification, ask any questions that he has regarding it, and then determine whether he wishes to submit a quotation on the product. The act of submitting the quotation should be interpreted by the buyer as an indication that the vendor is in a position to comply with the specifications.

MATERIAL SPECIFICATION

1. ITEM:

   Tiny Shrimp

2. DESCRIPTION:

   Small, cleaned, deveined, fresh frozen Indian shrimp—200 to 300 count per pound. Product to be cleaned and deveined, free of feelers, shells and extraneous matter. The texture must be firm and the color should be grey or pink.

3. PACKAGING:

   To be packed in 5-lb. quantities in poly bags with no staples used in the outer cartons. Outer carton must be 300 lb. test and have wax coating on exterior.

4. SPECIAL LABELING REQUIREMENTS:

   Labeling must be clear and legible, stating count and meeting all local, state and federal regulations.

5. CHEMICAL/BACTERIAL REQUIREMENTS:

   No off odors such as indole trimethylaime. The bacterial specifications are a maximum standard plate count of 100,000 a maximum coliform count of 10 grams, and E Coli count of less than 10 grams, salmonella negative, staph 10 gram maximum, coagulase positive, no staph present in 50 gram sample.

6. SPECIAL INSTRUCTIONS/REQUIREMENTS:

   Data sheets for bacteria analysis must accompany shipment of each lot.

Figure 16

There are two very important things to notice about this specification. First, the requirement that no staples are to be used in the outer packing cartons; and second, the heavy emphasis on bacterial requirements. The prohibition against staples results from the danger of staples being mixed in with the actual shrimp. The bacterial requirements are particularly stringent due to the very volatile nature of seafood, and due to the fact that this product is originating in a country where sanitary conditions may not be up to normally accepted U.S. standards.

It is far better to have a specification run too long than to abbreviate it and leave out some key piece of information which is needed to insure that the buyer receives the required quality.

MATERIAL SPECIFICATION

1. ITEM:

    #108 Rib

2. DESCRIPTION:

    The boned and tied, short cut, oven-prepared rib is the same as the over-prepared rib short cut item #107 remaining after the removal of the ribs, feather bones, back strap, and rib fingers. Boning procedures must be accomplished by scalping, thereby producing a smooth inner surface on the rib.

3. PACKAGING:

    The boneless rib must be tied to produce a firm, compact roast and must be held together by loops of strong twine uniformly spaced girth-wise and lengthwise around the outside of the roast.

4. SPECIAL LABELING REQUIREMENTS:

5. CHEMICAL/BACTERIAL REQUIREMENTS:

6. SPECIAL INSTRUCTIONS/REQUIREMENTS:

    Oven ready weight to be in a 26 to 28 lb. range.

Figure 17

This particular specification has been extracted from the Meat Buyer's Guide, published by the National Association of Meat Purveyors. It is rapidly becoming the standard specification reference book for people who buy meat products. You will note that in this particular specification (which in the Guide is accompanied by a picture of the particular cut) how the rib is to be trimmed is very clearly stated. This type of detail is essential if the buyer is to avoid a situation where the purveyor claims that he misunderstood what the buyer's requirements were.

USING THE PACKER'S SPECIFICATION

In some cases the buyer may even chose to use the packer's specification. This practice is particularly appropriate when the buyer is purchasing nationally branded merchandise. The only drawback to using it is the fact that the buyer is locking himself in to one particular manufacturer for as long as he specifies only that packer's label.

In recent years many restaurant operators have used an alternative form of the packer's specification by stating the packer's product and specification by name and then adding the words "or equivalent" at the end of the specification. Actually, the theory behind using a packer's specification is quite sound, since it is safe to assume that any manufacturer of widely accepted nationally branded merchandise has done sufficient research and development work on the product to permit the restaurateur to use it as his specification without fear of disappointment or inferior quality.

Relatively few food service establishments, for example, choose to develop their own specification for ketchup, simply because Heinz ketchup has developed a universal name and product acceptance. While there are numerous other brands of ketchup available to the food service industry, there is usually little argument regarding the quality of the Heinz product. As a result, food service operators can specify the Heinz product by brand name rather than taking the time to develop their own specification for ketchup. Many other products are also used as the specification for a particular product. Among them are Proctor and Gambels' Frymax shortening, General Foods' Jello, Sanka, and Maxwell House, Standard Brands' Royal gelatins and puddings, Hunt-Wesson's frying oil, Simplot's potatoes, and Hershey's and Nestles' cocoa powder.

PRODUCT VARIATIONS

Where specifications are particularly important, however, is when a product is taken from nature without much further processing. The best examples of this are the animal and fish protein items so important to every restaurant menu. Since broilers, shrimp, or hogs do not come out of an absolutely standard, uniform mold, there are always variations in size, shape, weight, color, and even texture when any of these products are purchased. It is these variations that can cause tremendous difficulty for the restaurant operator unless his specifications accurately and thoroughly spell out his requirements.

If he is buying bacon, his specification should state how many slices to the pound. If it is shrimp, they should state how many individual shrimp to the pound. In buying broilers for a chicken fry, he should state very carefully the weight of the bird he wants. If the chicken is to be cut up, he should specify the type of cut and number of pieces he expects. These specifications are particularly important, since they can have a very significant impact on the yield per broiler in a high volume food operation.

Specifications are absolutely essential for every food and supply item consumed in a food service operation. Sufficient work has been done in specification development to permit an operator to obtain them from his suppliers, and thus begin an operation with a fairly adequate set.

It is the operator's responsibility, however, to make this request. Few purveyors will automatically provide them. Once the operator has received an initial set of specifications from his purveyors (assuming he does not wish to develop them on his own), he can then begin to experiment through trial and error to decide which specifications are correct for his operation and which should be modified.

MENU CONSIDERATIONS: PRICE AND AVAILABILITY OF ITEMS

Another important aspect of purchasing is determining what menu offerings can reasonably be provided, considering both the price guidelines and the mix of different items which the menu must offer. There is no point in offering a selection of food products that are either volatile in price or uncertain in supply; the buyer will be unable to guarantee their availability. There is nothing more embarrassing for a restaurant operation than to list an item on the menu and then to have to inform the customer that the item ordered isn't available. (How many times have you been disappointed by the waiter who tells you, "We're terribly sorry but we don't have that item today"?)

In the case of many of the large national restaurant chains and contract feeding organizations, menu planning is done for a substantial period of time, so the actual printing of menus is only scheduled three to six times per year. As a result, any item included on these menus must be researched through the purchasing function to be sure that it will in fact be available at an affordable price for the entire period during which the particular menu is in effect.

The purchasing function should always be involved in the menu planning activity, not so much to determine a balanced menu as to evaluate the supply and price stability of each potential item during the menu period. For the more expensive restaurant that leans toward daily menu changes, this research is not as important, since each day's offerings can be adjusted to reflect what is currently available in the marketplace.

More often, however, a particular restaurant or contract feeder will establish a menu for some extended period of time and must therefore be reasonably confident of the availability and price of the items listed on the menu. Price is as important as availability in this regard, since if an item originally listed on the menu is $1.50 a pound and suddenly increases to $2.00 a pound, this can have a significant effect on the profitability of the operation.

Perhaps the best examples of what can happen are the many seafood houses which were severely injured during the early 1970's, when fresh seafood prices ran away from even the most farsighted menu planner. These prices put many of these restaurants in a situation which literally guaranteed them a loss with every order. The key point to remember here is that the menu offerings should be checked out thoroughly by the buyer before they are offered on the menu so that there will be a reasonable degree of certainty that these items will be available at affordable prices.

PHYSICAL CAPABILITIES OF AN OPERATION

Recognizing the physical capabilities of the facility is another consideration in purchasing. The square footage of available freezer and walk-in refrigerator space, the amount of preparation area available, and the type and sizes of cooking equipment in the kitchen: All will have an important bearing on the type of food purchased for the operation. A restaurant operation that relies exclusively on several ten-cubic-foot home freezers, for example, obviously cannot plan a menu based primarily on frozen food items. The current trend toward the increasing use of frozen foods in the restaurant industry has resulted in many redesign jobs for restaurants whose original freezer space became totally inadequate.

The buyer must therefore be very much aware of the physical limitations of the food service operation as he executes his buying activity. While he might like to take advantage of better purchase prices that are available to those who can buy in greater quantity, if his basic freezer capacity cannot hold such quantities without sharply reducing the number or amount of other items which it can hold, he has no choice but to forego such opportunities.

Similarly, if the preparation area in his particular operation is cramped and does not permit extensive in-house preparation of various food products, he has no choice but to purchase prepared foods such as a completed veal stroganoff, rather than the individual ingredients needed to make such an item within the restaurant. Recognizing that the physical capabilities of the unit must influence the food buying program, the buyer should keep these physical capabilities clearly in mind and tailor his buying program specifically to them.

VENDOR DELIVERY

An obvious outgrowth of the storage capacities of the operation is the type of delivery required from vendors. A unit with very limited storage capacity (both frozen and refrigerated) will require frequent delivery from its vendors. Since delivery expenses are one of the most rapidly increasing charges in the food service marketplace, there is a direct correlation between frequency of delivery and the price charged by the vendor. Under ideal conditions, the buyer should aim for once-a-week delivery of frozen and dry merchandise, and twice-a-week delivery of refrigerated items such as butter, eggs and cheese, and produce. Freshly baked goods should be targeted for delivery twice a week, but if an occasional third delivery is required to insure freshness of the product, it should be scheduled.

Special delivery requirements are occasionally unavoidable, but they should be kept to an absolute minimum, since they raise food costs. A reputable vendor with whom you have had a good business relationship will accept an occasional request for an emergency or special delivery. However, if these requests assume any frequency at all, he will quickly react by either adding a special charge for these deliveries, or by increasing his overall selling price to you. This rate will increase geometrically when these deliveries are required at night or on weekends.

Good planning will usually enable you to avoid all but emergency situations where special deliveries are required. Remember: Deliveries cost money. The more often you ask your vendor to deliver, the more he will charge for the product he is supplying to you.

SHELF LIFE

Another factor that must be kept in mind by the buyer as he prepares his food buying program is the shelf life that can be expected of the various items used in the operation. Obviously, if most of the foods purchased are in the frozen or canned state, shelf life is really not a major problem. Depending upon their particular makeup, frozen foods have a shelf life of anywhere from two months to one year or more if they remain below zero degrees Fahrenheit. Naturally, the only time a restaurant operator would want to hold a product for extended periods of time would be when his original cost was so far below the anticipated future market price that such prolonged holding would contribute comparative cost reduction opportunities.

The most frequent source of trouble is refrigerated goods, especially the dairy products and fresh produce. Under ideal conditions these products will normally store well for up to a week or more. However, since it is frequently difficult to know precisely how long these products have been in storage before they are received at your location, blanket assumptions that they all have a built-in week or more of storage potential can sometimes be very dangerous. For this reason, as well as for a number of other quality reasons, incoming inspection of all merchandise delivered by vendors is absolutely vital. In the case of fresh produce, a quick check into each case of lettuce, celery, or tomatoes will frequently reveal those items which have seen their maximum storage capacity and are on the verge of a significant quality deterioration. If the user does not take steps to inspect merchandise at the time of delivery, he has no one to blame but himself if it goes bad shortly after delivery.

DEVELOPING A BASIC BUYING PLAN

Purchasing Meat, Poultry, and Seafood

Probably the most important area of procurement for any food service or restaurant operation is the purchase of meat. The ultimate profitability of the operation could easily depend on how well the meat is purchased. The National Live Stock and Meat Board has recently published a hardcover volume entitled *Meat in the Food Service Industry,* which provides excellent insight into the overall use of meat in food service with particular emphasis on meat procurement. This 80-page volume is available from the National Live Stock and Meat Board, 36 South Wabash Ave., Chicago, Illinois 60603, at a price of approximately $8.00.

Two other volumes which are helpful to the meat buyer are the *Meat Buyer's Guide to Standardized Meat Cuts,* and the *Meat Buyer's Guide to Portion Control Meat Cuts.* Both are published by the National Association of Meat Purveyors, 252 West Ina Road, Tuscon, Arizona 85704.

These volumes are an excellent overall guideline for the effective purchase of meat products. They describe in both words and with full-color photographs each of the various cuts of beef, pork, veal, and lamb which a food service operator is likely to purchase. In addition to being fully described and illustrated, each of these cuts is assigned a number which is nationally recognized by all reputable meat vendors, and which may be used by the buyer in specifying the particular cut he wishes to purchase. By instituting a nationwide absolutely uniform set of specifications on meat products, the National Association of Meat Purveyors has eliminated a major source of buyer-vendor misunderstanding and abuse. Every buyer of meat products should have a copy of one or both of these volumes on the desk. Their cost will be repaid many times over during just the first week or two of their use. Information on them may be obtained from your local NAMP member.

In the case of poultry and seafood, the buyer should take advantage of existing government specifications on the various items which he requires. He should also ask his potential suppliers for copies of specifications which they would recommend to their customers. The supplier is often in the best position to recommend a specification on a particular item. The buyer is obviously under no obligation to accept this recommended specification if he feels it is not right for his operation. However, suppliers that have been in business for many years are probably more familiar with product requirements and therefore in a better position to recommend various specifications than anyone else with whom you do business. Consequently, it is to your advantage to utilize the knowledge of these suppliers as you develop your operating specifications. Naturally, you can modify these specifications at any time that you feel they fail to perform in your operation.

In using government specifications, the buyer is taking advantage of specifications that have been developed over an extended period of time by the combined agencies of the federal government. While these specifications may seem unwieldy at times, generally they include the most important characteristics of each of the products they cover and can be used as a general guideline for developing more particular specifications for each individual food service or restaurant operation.

Another method you might consider to help determine which products to buy is to adopt the specifications that are "commonly used in the industry." This simply means contacting potential suppliers and asking them to furnish you with copies of the specifications that are most commonly used by other organizations in the restaurant and food service industry. It is to the supplier's advantage to make certain that most of his customers use the same set of specifications, since he can carry fewer products to service all their needs. So you can expect the supplier to respond positively to any request for copies of such specifications.

When requesting such specifications from a supplier, the buyer has the added safety of knowing that many other buyers are presently working with these exact specifications. This fact in itself should provide more than enough assurance to the buyer that the item being specified will be the proper quality for his operation. Obviously, if it is not, he can then use the "industry specifications" as a starting point from which to develop his own.

Delivery Schedules

Another area that the buyer should consider before making any purchase commitments is the type of delivery schedule he wishes to utilize. This must also take into account the delivery capabilities of the purveyors with whom he will be negotiating. A recent study of food purchasing procedures conducted by the Bureau of Business Research at Indiana State University showed that in a survey of sixty operators, the average number of orders placed was 21½ per week, and the average number of suppliers used was 11 per week. The study went on to point out that the average unit spent 1.4 hours per day checking and storing an average of five deliveries per day. This amounted to an average of 17 minutes that were spent checking in each order.

While on the surface these statistics may seem rather bland, they point up a key area for improvement in most food service operations: the cost of ordering and receiving. Each order costs money to place and to receive. This cost not only accrues to the buyer whose personnel must spend time on both ends of the order, but also, and perhaps more importantly, to the vendor, who must likewise spend time and money receiving, filling, delivering, and billing each order. Hence, it becomes rather elementary that the fewer the number of orders that can be placed each week, and the larger their individual size, the lower will be the cost devoted to order placement and receipt. Since the vendor also benefits from these less frequent but larger orders, the buyer should look to the vendor to pass these savings on to him in the form of a lower price.

While storage capacities obviously play a part in determining the size and frequency of your orders, you should maximize the size of each order and lengthen the time between orders to whatever degree is possible within market and product quality considerations. Product shelf life must also be considered in determining how long an item is to be held in storage before it is consumed. It is fairly common for certain large multi-unit food service operations to purchase and store up to a year's supply of a given commodity in order to protect themselves against price increases or supply shortages. However, these decisions must be made with a careful eye on the financial impact that such long-term storage will have on the firm's balance sheet and with the same care and consideration as for the opportunity buy.

One-Stop Shopping

During the past few years the concept of one-stop shopping has become very popular in the food service industry. Under this concept the food service operator is offered an opportunity to purchase a maximum number of his operating requirements from one source. He may be able to purchase his meat, poultry, seafood, vegetable and dairy products, as well as his paper goods and operating supplies from one company. This company makes one delivery per week covering all of the aforementioned items. The advantages to the food service operator from this type of system are obvious: He is able to maximize his purchase volume with one purveyor and to sharply reduce the number (and the expense) of deliveries received at his establishment each week.

Some purveyors serving the food service industry have carried the concept even further, to the point where they also offer kitchen equipment, menus, and even interior decorating services as a part of their one-stop shopping package. In addition, the one-stop shopping purveyor is usually in a position to offer a menu planning and inventory-scheduling service, which will not only assist the operator in determining the mix of products to be offered on his menu, but will also assist him in scheduling his purchase requirements. To the small or intermediate operator who cannot afford his own in-house staff to provide these important services, their availability from the one-stop shopping purveyor can be most significant.

While this concept has been tested with mixed results in a number of major metropolitan areas across the country over the last five years, it is my opinion that the one-stop shopping concept makes great sense for the smaller food service operator who needs every opportunity he can muster to maximize his procurement volume.

In the case of the larger chains, especially those with their own manufacturing or commissary facilities, the one-stop shopping concept offers correspondingly fewer values simply because the purchasing leverage already inherent in the chain's operation tends to defeat many of the economies otherwise available through the one-stop shopping system. However, the small and intermediate size operator should not discount the significant savings available in the areas of order placement and order receiving. By placing one order each week for this broad spectrum of products and worrying about only one delivery for all his products, the food service operator greatly reduces the time spent on the ordering and delivering function, thus freeing his time for more important applications to the operation of the business.

Preparation Time and Steps

The reconstitution steps and time required to convert the product which he is buying into a table ready menu offering must also be considered in a basic buying plan. During the past five years, because of the development of frozen prepared entree items, the food service industry has gone through a remarkable renaissance in product use patterns. While many of the better quality food service establishments have shunned these new products as being "beneath our dignity and quality standards," these products are in fact the new generation of foods for the food service industry.

Analyze the benefits of using these products and discuss them thoroughly with your associates in the food service establishment before you determine whether they should replace certain products presently being purchased for the operation.

Although each specific food product may have to be approached from a slightly different procurement point of view, the fundamental purchasing philosophies and techniques outlined in these six chapters can be applied on essentially a universal level. Once the buyer knows exactly what he wishes to purchase, he then seeks out the vendors best qualified to fill that need, and negotiates the most favorable price, delivery, and payment terms possible. There, in one sentence, we have the essence of purchasing for the food service industry.

Yet even recognizing the importance of purchasing and its effects of profit, many buyers will continue to do things the "easy" way. Unfortunately, this may not be simply "easy," but sloppy and a drain on profits as well. The Indiana State University study referred to earlier showed that among the sixty food service operators surveyed, "the bulk of the orders were placed without the use of specifications or written ordering procedures. Two-thirds of the orders were placed by telephone." These findings suggest continued room for substantial improvement in purchasing techniques in the food service industry.

Chapter 6 Questions

1. What information should be included in the specification for a food product?

2. To what degree should receiving procedures be covered in the specification?

3. Why should the purchasing department participate in menu planning activities?

4. How does the physical layout and equipment of the food service operation impact on its buying plan?

5. In what way should the buyer concern himself with delivery arrangements?

6. How do product shelf life and reconstitution time influence purchasing decisions?

7

Portion Control and Frozen Prepared Food Items

A DEFINITION

As described previously, specifications are the starting point for the purchase of any items. In the case of portion control and frozen prepared food items, specifications are even more important, because the product purchased will probably be the product presented on the plate to the customer.

Before beginning an in-depth consideration of these very important and rapidly growing factors in the restaurant industry, perhaps we should take a few moments for a definition of terms. *Portion control* simply means a product whose portion size is predetermined in some way to insure that each customer receives precisely the same amount of food. Common industry terminology usually designates portion control for those items which are prepared at some place other than the actual place of consumption. However, I have found that this is a somewhat misleading designation, since portion control often exists at the location where the product is being consumed, even though the product may not have been received at that location in a portion control condition. Thus, portion control items may be either those that are prepared at another location, or those that are prepared at the consuming location so that portion control will result. For the purpose of this book, we will define portion control foods as those which, like frozen prepared foods, are prepared at another location and merely need to be reconstituted (a fancy word for reheated) at the point of ultimate consumption.

Over the past five years, the usage of such foods has increased significantly in the restaurant and contract feeding industries. The first half of the 1970's can truly be termed the years of the precooked meal, although many restaurant operators and restaurant patrons dislike that term. Actually, a precooked meal that is properly prepared, frozen, stored, reconstituted, and properly served can be every bit as good as any fresh, prepared-to-order meal. In fact, in many ways it is superior to the prepared-to-order meal, because the prepared-to-order meal may frequently be ordered at a time when the kitchen staff and the food inventory are not right for that particular order. In those instances, it may be prepared in a hurried fashion, may be given less than the full attention of the chef and other kitchen staff members, or may be made with some essential ingredients left out. When this happens, the supposedly fresh, prepared-to-order entree item may turn out to be a disappointment for the customer.

When a frozen prepared food item is purchased, however, assuming that the manufacturer has adequate quality standards, all that the serving establishment has to do is properly reconstitute and serve the item. While not every frozen prepared food item can carry the banner of quality equal to those prepared on-the-spot for immediate consumption, many such frozen prepared items can compete most effectively with prepared-to-order food.

As with any other food item, specifications are a prerequisite to the purchase of any frozen prepared (portion control) food item. Unless the user has such large volume requirements that he is able to interest a manufacturer in producing a product specifically to his requirements, he will have to content himself with accepting the specification of an existing manufacturer. Many of the large institutional distributors have reached the volume level where they are able to have frozen prepared food items manufactured to their specifications and put under their label for ultimate sale to their customers. In these situations the individual operator is able to rely on the purchasing power, quality control expertise, and fundamental product development talents of the distributor who has selected particular items to put under his own label. Since the distributor is trying to satisfy the needs of many customers, you can assume that he has assembled a good line of products. When considering the use of frozen prepared foods that are offered as a part of a distributor's line, the individual operator and small chain should remember that they are hitchhiking on the larger volume requirements that the distributor can utilize in having this product manufactured expressly for him. In no way would the individual operator and small chain be able to develop such volume requirements on their own or have such products ordinarily avaliable to them.

The individual operator should recognize the potential reduction in cost and improved efficiency that can result from the selective use of frozen prepared (portion control) foods. This is not an advocacy for the total use of these products in the restaurant or contract feeding business. It is, however, a strong recommendation that the operator consider a balance of both frozen prepared foods and foods that are prepared to order on a daily basis as the optimum.

Perhaps the two greatest advantages to using such products are 1) greater menu diversity, and 2) considerable savings in kitchen work time and hence expense. How many restaurants, for example, could normally afford to offer dishes such as chicken cordon bleu, chicken kiev, veal marengo, and baked halibut in cheese sauce on a regular menu basis if they were to be prepared from scratch for each order? Obviously, the answer is very few. Even in those few restaurants that might chose to offer one or two special items each day, the inclusion of one or more of these would require a certain amount of guess work on the part of the manager and the chef as to the number of portions of each item customers will order at each meal period.

Once this guess had been made, the necessary raw materials would have to be assembled, and at least the preliminary preparation activities would have to get underway. If the guess was absolutely correct, there would be just the right amount of raw materials and hence finished portions to correspond with customer orders. However, the chances of such a guess being exactly right are quite remote. Thus the restaurant would face the prospect of either having too little or too much of the particular item available and of doing most of the preperation while the guest is sitting at the table (sometimes quite impatiently) waiting to be served.

How much simpler would it be to include one or more of such items on the menu with the knowledge (and perhaps the menu designation) that they are prepared at an earlier date and frozen for reconstitution at the point of use. By so doing, the management of the operation is not required to prepare a specific number of portions until the orders for these portions have actually been received. Then, with the use of a combination of microwave and convection ovens, the reconstitution process can be completed in relatively short time, and the operator can serve his guest without the uncertainties of anticipating his needs and hoping that his estimates work out properly.

The use of portion control or frozen prepared foods allows greater predictability for the individual food service operation. This in turn very directly affects the purchasing function. Since most of the frozen prepared items which an operation uses are regular inventory stock for major distributors, there is usually little difficulty in obtaining replenishment supplies on very short notice. Hence, the buyer for the food service operation knows with a fair degree of certainty that if a particular item is put on the menu, he will be able to maintain a continuous supply, regardless of the number of customers who order the item.

Furthermore, since these items are frozen, they can be stored for extended periods when necessary. Thus the buyer can time his purchases to take advantage of fluctuations in the market price. Perhaps the best example of such flexibility is with the more popular seafood items such as shrimp, scallops, and rock lobster tails. Although these items do require minimal preparation at the point of consumption, purchasing them in the frozen state eliminates the considerable cleaning work that would be required if they were purchased fresh, to say nothing of the substantial yield loss during the initial processing stage.

In addition, a buyer who purchases these items in the frozen state can take advantage of the substantial price fluctuations which normally occur during the course of any twelve-month period. Naturally, if the buyer wishes to be especially conservative, he will purchase one-twelfth of his requirements during each of the twelve calendar months, thereby insuring that he will pay no more than an average of the annual price.

However, if he has watched the past record of the price fluctuations on these three very popular seafood items and has discussed anticipated future price movements with his seafood suppliers, he will most likely be in a position where he will develop a feel for the market price and can therefore take advantage of the temporary periods of special price attractiveness. By doing this, he will purchase anywhere from one to four or more month's supply of the particular item. If he were purchasing these items on a fresh basis only, he would have no opportunity to make this type of market judgment, since the perishability of the item would require that he buy fresh stocks every two or three days and pay the current market price each time he purchased them. Hence, the use of the frozen item opens up a significant opportunity for price reductions that would not be available with the use of fresh products. While the type of price fluctuation frequently seen in the shrimp, scallops, and rock lobster tail markets is not as evident in some of the beef and poultry based frozen prepared food items, there are still price opportunities based on market timing available with these items.

EQUIPMENT CONSIDERATIONS FOR PORTION CONTROL ITEMS

There are three equipment considerations that must be made when a restaurant or contract feeding operation intends to rely heavily on frozen prepared foods (portion control items). The first and the most obvious is an expanded freezer space to accommodate the disproportionate amount of frozen merchandise that will be coming into the operation. If an adequate amount of such space (with good refrigeration controls and proper ventilation) does not already exist, expansion of the freezer capacity will probably be necessary before such a program can begin.

The next consideration is whether you have or can purchase a microwave oven. This can be used for a combination of defrosting and browning activities. The major microwave oven manufacturers have published extensive sets of directions for the optimum use of their products with frozen prepared food items. However, the microwave oven should be considered more as a defrosting mechanism than as the ultimate cooking device. Cooking should be left to another piece of equipment and the third consideration—a good convection oven.

A convection oven is simply the traditional oven that is upgraded by adding a fan to circulate the air during the baking process. After frozen food has been defrosted and partially cooked in the microwave oven, it can be transferred to the convection oven for the final browning and finishing off process prior to being served to the guest.

Clearly, the use of frozen prepared/portion control food greatly increases the flexibility of the food service operation and allows for a much more varied menu for guests. However, using these products without any personal touch on the part of the kitchen staff can result in a somewhat stereotyped and sterile food operation. If you take the time to work out a reasonable mixture of frozen prepared food items as well as items produced from scratch on the day of consumption, you should have the proper balance and harmony for a successful and well-run restaurant operation.

Chapter 7 Questions

1. What does the designation "portion control" mean to you?

2. What factors do you think contributed to the sharp increase in the use of frozen prepared entrees during the first half of the 1970's?

3. How can the small operator best obtain frozen prepared entree items?

4. In evaluating the possible use frozen prepared entrees in a food service operation, what factors should the buyer consider?

5. Discuss the differences in handling procedures between frozen prepared foods and regular, prepared-to-order items.

8

The Purchase of Alcoholic Beverages

ALCOHOLIC BEVERAGES

One of the most misunderstood and frequently neglected segments of the food service purchasing spectrum is the procurement of alcoholic beverages. Since those establishments with liquor licenses normally expect that liquor will bring in anywhere from 25 to 50 percent of their total sales dollars, and since liquor normally produces a 70 to 75 percent gross profit (as compared with a 40 to 60 percent gross profit from food), the importance of careful and thorough purchasing of liquor cannot be stressed enough. A restaurant operator should devote as much, if not more, time to his liquor buying as he does to his food items. (See Figure 18.)

One of the greatest frustrations facing the liquor buyer is the fact that no matter how good a negotiator he may be, there is a fixed price, established by individual state law, at which liquor is sold. These laws, which vary according to state, leave no grounds for legitimate negotiation with regard to individual selling prices. Neither do they reflect in any way the relative volume requirements of various liquor consuming installations. Thus, a fifty seat, family owned and operated restaurant can purchase liquor at the same price as a chain with 150 installations in that state that collectively consume two to

Liquor Vs. Food
Cost & Gross Profit Comparisons

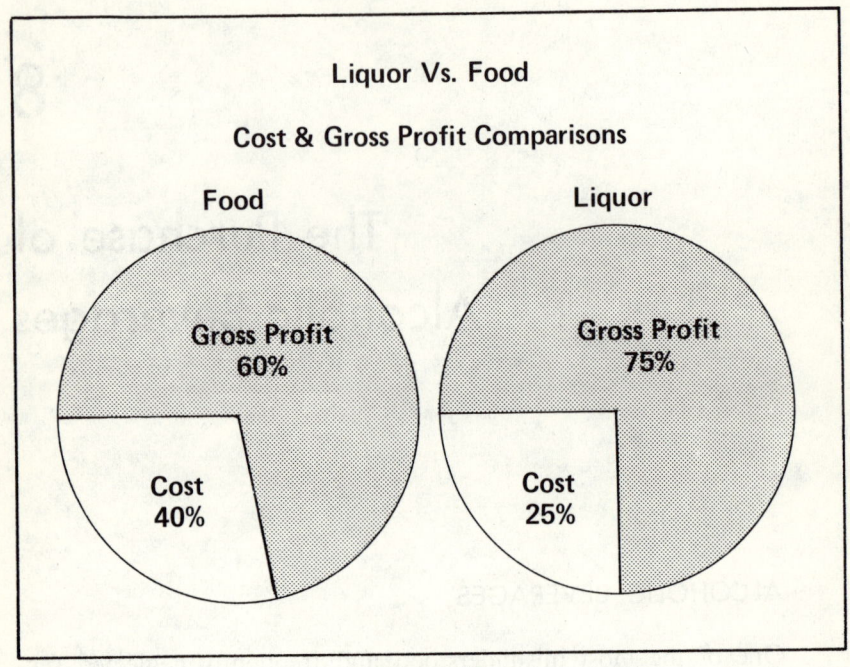

Food
- Gross Profit 60%
- Cost 40%

Liquor
- Gross Profit 75%
- Cost 25%

Figure 18

three hundred times as much liquor as the individual operation. The liquor companies seem to share the frustration of not being able to extend price concessions to large purchasers. However, the state laws are extremely inflexible on this point, and a case of quarts of a given brand of scotch is priced the same for all purchasers, regardless of size and rate of consumption. (See Figure 19.)

POSTOFFS

In many states, however, there is an opportunity for the astute restaurant buyer to improve the price at which he purchases his liquor requirements.

The term *postoff* is used in the liquor industry to describe periodic price reductions or free goods promotions which are offered by the distillers to their customers. Liquor prices are traditionally published or posted on a monthly basis, and since these special prices

CONTROL (MONOPOLY) STATES

Alabama	Mississippi	Ohio
Idaho	Montana	Oregon
Iowa	New Hampshire	Pennsylvania
Maine	North Carolina	Utah
Michigan		Vermont

The states listed above operate under a set of state liquor laws wherein the state itself is the seller of liquor to the public. Any purchaser buying liquor for food service establishments in one of these states should consult his local state alcoholic beverage authority for applicable rules. If he has any further questions he can contact the Distilled Spirits Council of the United States, Incorporated, 1300 Pennsylvania Building, Washington, D.C. 20004. This organization publishes a summary of state laws and regulations relating to distilled spirits.

Figure 19

are reductions off normal selling prices, the terminology "postoff" came into common usage as a means of describing them.

The postoff can take the form of an outright price reduction, such as when a given distiller offers Scotch brand X at a reduction of $6.00 per case of 12 quarts from his normal selling price of $72.00 per case. This is a price reduction of 8.3% and may be available for all purchases of that brand during a period ranging from two to six weeks. Normally the distiller will repeat the offer two or three times per year. Or the postoff can be an offer to customers of a buying incentive in the form of free goods connected with a volume purchase. The distiller might offer one case of gin free with each purchase of 10 cases during a four week period. In this case, the free goods amount to a 9% price reduction, since the purchaser is receiving eleven cases of product for the amount normally paid for 10 cases.

The key factor in utilizing the postoff system as a buying tool is the buyer's anticipating the availability of various postoff promotions and timing his purchasing activity accordingly. If he knows that product X will be on postoff during a four week period every 90 days, he should attempt to schedule his buying of that particular product only during those periods.

Although evaluating the mix and rate of consumption of various liquor products is not a buyer's direct responsibility, he should nevertheless work closely with the operations people in his establishment to evaluate these all-important issues. There should be a direct correlation between the specific brands purchased and their rate of request by customers. If a particular brand of liquor is consumed at a rate of less than one or two bottles per week, you would probably have good reason to question whether this particular brand should be stocked at all. Since liquor cannot generally be purchased in less than full case lots, a slow moving item may represent a serious inventory excess. The operator must always remember that once he purchases a product, he has money tied up in it. If that product does not sell, therefore, these funds are not working for him.

SELECT RESPONSIBLE DISTRIBUTORS

A key factor for the liquor purchaser is to select distributors on whom he can depend for accurate and up-to-date merchandising information, including near-term promotions which will have an impact on his net purchases. Although there are severe limitations on the services which a distributor can provide to a purchaser, the buyer should attempt to establish a rapport with a select number of distributors whom he can turn to for those services which are permitted by law. Among the services which a distributor salesman can provide are advice in the selection of a product mix, recommendations regarding order patterns and order quantities, special delivery arrangements, assistance in merchandising and promotion, and recommendations about new products. Each of these things can have an impact on the effectiveness and hence the profitability of the operations liquor service.

LIQUOR BRANDS

Another question which buyers of liquor have to confront is that of which brand to buy. Should he purchase the nationally known brand names, or should he purchase the lesser known regional or local brands of the same proof which frequently cost anywhere from $10.00 to $30.00 less per case? Please note the insertion "of the same proof." There is no legitimate comparison between 86 proof nationally known brand of scotch and an 80 proof local brand. Any establishment attempting to substitute the latter for the former is not only misleading its customers, but is also running the risk of turning them away because of inferior merchandise. However, there is a legitimate case to be made for substituting a local or regional brand for a nationally branded item of the same proof where the customer does not request a specific product by brand name.

It is common practice in the restaurant industry to divide brands of liquor into two categories: the *call brands* and the *pour brands*. The call brands refer to those nationally branded products which are usually specified by name when a customer orders a drink; i.e., Black & White on the rocks, a Beefeater martini, or Canadian Club and water. The pour brands, on the other hand, are those brands that are normally used when the customer does not specify a particular brand name; i.e., a scotch and water or a vodka martini. The designation *pour brand* is also frequently interchanged with the designation *well brand*, which has its derivation from the fact that these products are normally kept in the serving wells located just beneath the top surface of the bar so that they are readily accessible to the bartender. The call brands (those requested by name) are usually prominently displayed across the back of the bar where they can be readily seen and selected by the customers.

Service bars (bars that are located so that patrons do not have to be physically present while their drinks are being made) usually use pour brands. If a customer requests a particular brand, however, it is the operator's responsibility to be sure that either the customer gets the brand he requests or he be told that it is not available. This is particularly important since, if a waiter accepts an order for Johnny Walker red on the rocks and then delivers a house brand, he is violating the law.

ORDERING THE PROPER MIX OF BRANDS

The person purchasing the liquor can make a substantial contribution to the efficiency of the liquor buying program by making sure that the proper mix of call brands and pour brands is ordered for the establishment. There is no point in using nationally known (and generally more expensive) brands when less expensive products of equal proof are available. It is not the province of this text to debate the merits of nationally branded products versus their regional or local counterparts of similar proof. However, as a result of extensive testing in a number of food service establishments, I have found that once the bottle is removed from view, assuming the proof is the same, a good quality local or regional brand can perform at much the same quality as a national brand. Naturally, each individual restaurant or food service operator must take these decisions for himself. However, in view of the twenty to fourty percent savings which are available through local or regional lines, the person responsible for buying liquor for an establishment should certainly weigh these savings heavily before ordering national brands.

A final comment regarding liquor purchasing: There is no excuse for compromising quality. If a particular brand is clearly inferior in taste to a more expensive brand, it should not be purchased under any circumstances. Similarly, you should never substitute one brand for another of a higher proof. This is akin to removing a chopped steak made from top sirloin from the menu and substituting a chopped steak made from ground beef with the belief that the two will be directly comparable. Because of the excellent markup on all alcoholic beverages, there is no excuse for cutting corners. As costs go up, it is far better for the operator to raise his selling prices than to reduce the quality of the merchandise he is serving to his guests. There will always be a cheaper product around, but the question is, what is the price/value relationship of that cheaper product compared with the more expensive, but infinitely better quality product it is replacing?

WINES

Over the past five years there has been a tremendous growth in the popularity of wines in the restaurant industry. A restaurant that chooses to offer a selection of the vintage domestic and imported wines should take this task very seriously. This will probably involve engaging the services of a wine expert to plan the wine list and to recommend methods of procurement to help build the wine cellar. This is not a task for amateurs, so the person responsible for the buying should enlist professional assistance in the purchase of wines.

The great growth in wine consumption can be attributed in part to the availability of carafe or decanter wines that are generally the less expensive varieties that are purchased in half gallon or gallon jugs. While these wines are always considerably less expensive than the fine vintage wines, it is important not to purchase wines of such inferior quality that the guests will be disappointed with them. There are many fine quality domestic wines available in the half gallon and gallon sizes, and these products lend themselves extremely well to a modestly priced carafe wine program. Unfortunately, there are also wines sold in these larger containers that are of borderline quality. As such, they have no place in a carafe wine program.

One surprising fact is that the difference in price between a case of these fine quality wines in one gallon jugs and a case of some demonstrably inferior product is frequently as little as $2.00 or $3.00 per case. However, the difference between their respective qualities is so extreme that one wonders why, for a saving of $2.00 to $3.00 per case, such poor quality selection would be offered. However, these are the considerations that the buyer should keep in mind when he considers purchasing wine for a carafe program. In my experience, I have found it far better to increase the price of the carafe to maintain the desired gross profit on a quality product than it is to reduce the quality of the purchase in order to save a few dollars per case.

LIQUOR DISTRIBUTORS

The selection of the liquor distributor is a critical factor in any procurement programs. Since liquor prices are controlled by state law, and all distributors are required to sell at the same price, selection of a distributor should be made solely on the basis of the service which the distributor renders. Important items in the service category are consistency of delivery schedules, willingness to accommodate special emergency orders, bookkeeping procedures and records, and merchanding assistance in the form of promotional material, new product information, and assisting with special requests such as occasional displays.

Many distributors carry the same brands of liquor. Sometimes, however, a particular brand is exclusively carried by one distributor. In such cases the buyer must decide how important that particular brand is, whether he wishes to add that particular distributor to his vendor list, or whether he prefers instead to get along without that particular brand. As a general rule of thumb, the buyer should try to avoid having more than three distributors. Bookkeeping and receiving problems multiply with each additional distributor servicing the account. Hence, in the interest of better control and minimum bookkeeping expense, a smaller number of distributors should be used. It is my experience that a combination of three broadly based distributors will be sufficient for most restaurant operations.

When entering into a business relationship with a distributor, the buyer should call in a responsible representative of the firm (preferably one of the firm's officers) and state very clearly the ground rules under which he expects to do business. This conversation should include the nature of the relationships which he expects the distributor's personnel to have with the employees of his restaurant. Since distributor sales personnel frequently provide free samples of the products to induce customer volume, the buyer should specify carefully any prohibitions which his firm has in this area.

This initial meeting should also cover in detail the delivery services required and the type of bookkeeping procedures which the distributor will provide. The buyer should also explain to the distributor the type of operation he runs. This way, the distributor can better understand the needs of the customer and the range of products and services which his customer expects. If a wine program is to be a part of the operation, the buyer should be sure to select distributors who can supply a broad range of labels to satisfy the needs of a good wine program.

The meeting should also cover very carefully the firm's desires to maximize use of the postoff system in their buying activities. The distributor should be asked to present a recommended program to the buyer outlining the way this postoff system could best be utilized. By requiring such recommendations from several distributors, the buyer can quickly compare the efficiency of each distributor by going over their proposals. Since the liquor distributor does not have price incentives to offer as a reason for selecting his firm as a vendor, special attention should be paid to the other services which are available from each distributor.

One last word: Because distributors are so tightly restricted in their pricing alternatives by the individual state liquor laws, there seems to be more of a propensity in this particular trade group for offering cash rebates and other emoluments which are not allowed by various state liquor laws. Many distributors justify their participation in this practice on competitive grounds, stating that, "If everyone else is doing it and I fail to go along, I will lose business to my competitors."

It is not my purpose to pass on the morality of the liquor distributing industry, but simply to alert the buyer who is interested in doing the best possible job for his firm not to succumb to the cash offers which are frequently available from liquor distributors. It is to the buyer's best interest to take maximum advantage of postoffs and special free goods promotions. However, he should be very careful not to step over the line and participate in any activities which are outside the state liquor laws. If the buyer has any doubts regarding the propriety of a particular practice being suggested by the distributor, a call to his local state liquor authority will quickly resolve the question.

Chapter 8 Questions

1. Discuss the reasons why the purchase of alcoholic beverages should receive special attention from the buyer for the food service establishment.

2. Define and discuss the postoff system of liquor merchandising.

3. How can the buyer best adopt the postoff system to his own needs?

4. Discuss the use of brand name versus pour brand items.

5. What are some of the advantages of a carafe wine program?

6. In establishing a business relationship with a liquor distributor, what points should be covered at the initial meeting?

9

The Purchase of Tabletop Items and Operating Supplies

TABLETOP AND OPERATING EXPENSES

In many restaurant operations the procurement of both tabletop items (any nonedible item which must be placed on top of the table in order to facilitate or complement the meal service) and operating supplies (soaps, mops, brushes and pots and pans) is an area that is either overlooked entirely or treated secondarily. In most restaurant operations the combined expenditure for these two categories should not exceed 3–4% of total annual sales. Naturally, during the first year that a restaurant is in operation, these expenditures will run to a considerably higher percentage of sales due to their high initial cost. However, once this initial cost has been incurred (many companies consider the initial expenditure for tabletop items and operating supplies to be a capital expense and, hence, one to be depreciated in much the same way as a dishwashing machine or a convection oven), the annual expenditure should not exceed 1–2% of gross sales for tabletop items and 2% for operating supplies.

The buyer should check to see if these expenditures in his particular operation conform with this general guideline. If it is running substantially below, then the company is not meeting its ongoing needs in these areas and is probably short-changing its guests. If the expenditures are running substantially above this level, then either the buyer is not exercising maximum purchasing efficiency or there is sufficient product loss, either through overuse or disappearance, to warrant a very careful investigation. Either of these conditions may be caused by using the wrong item for a specific application.

TABLETOP ITEMS

Tabletop items include dishware of all types, glasses, flatware (both stainless or silverplate), serving accessories such as salt and pepper shakers, ashtrays, coffee and teapots, salad dressing dispensers and the like, tablecloths and napkins, and other table accessories such as candles, menu holders, wine lists, etc. Depending upon the type of restaurant operation we might also find such items as placemats and paper napkins included in this category.

In both these areas, the small operation will differ considerably from the larger operation in its purchasing methods. The small restaurant operation should locate and choose a local supply house that offers good service and can meet its needs. During the initial stages of locating such a supply house, the buyer should interview at least three different organizations to determine which one is best qualified to cover his requirements and provide the type of service which he is seeking. During these prepurchase interviews the buyer should state very clearly what he will need in terms of delivery frequency, type of merchandise, order lead time, credit requirements, requests for special items that are not normally held in the suppliers stock, etc. If this is clearly spelled out, the buyer should be able to make a decision fairly quickly on which organization is best equipped to supply him.

Once the supplier selection has been made, it is best to purchase all tabletop items through the one supply company. This is not to suggest that all orders for all merchandise ever required should be directed to the one supplier. However, the price differentials on the purchase volume of a small restaurant operation are not large enough to warrant constant competitive bidding each time merchandise is required. The small operator might instead interview the perspective supplier with the understanding that the firm chosen would receive the *majority* of his business for a period of up to twelve months. By offering this "carrot" to the perspective suppliers, the buyer may be able to obtain better price and service guarantees than his volume would normally justify.

A different set of considerations faces the buyer for the large chain operation. Here his tabletop supply purchases may run into hundreds of thousands of dollars per year and should justify a totally different approach to the procurement of these items. In this situation, the buyer should first consider the basic specifications for the tabletop items he plans to use to be sure that he is requesting an item which can be made by a number of manufacturers.

For example, a given chain may specify a particular shape of china. Unbeknownst to them, this china is manufactured by only one china company. A buyer who allows this specification to take precedence is giving that one mill an exclusive on his business. This not only removes any possibility of price competition, but also eliminates an alternate source of supply should the primary supplier suddenly be unwilling or unable to fill his supply commitment. Examples of this type of situation are quite common in the restaurant industry. I am aware of a number of situations where major restaurant operations have severely restricted themsleves by utilizing a particular shape, design, weight, texture, or color of tabletop item that is available from only one supplier. In most of these cases such action is rationalized on aesthetic grounds, and while that may be of some validity, I still consider any item that is available from only a single source to be an unacceptable business condition.

Overseas Purchasing

Another possibility that the larger operation can take advantage of is purchasing merchandise overseas. Frequently a buyer can save up to 20% on items such as flatware that is manufactured and purchased in the Far East. If a buyer decides to follow this course, he should not attempt to carry out these overseas negotiations on a direct basis. Because of the many pitfalls involved in dealing in foreign markets, a vendor experienced in this area should be employed to handle not only the initial negotiations, but also the myriad of details involved in the actual importation of the merchandise at a later date. Such considerations as import duties, customs inspections, use of bonded warehouses, and the like are enough to boggle the mind of the average buyer and to consume inordinate amounts of his already valuable time. The vendor who can be utilized in this situation will expect his normal markup on the transaction. However, since the base price is lower, a fee of this type is well worth spending to insure the smooth and harmonious purchase and flow of the product.

Stockless Purchasing

For all food service operations spending in excess of $100,000 per year for tabletop items, a commonly used purchasing technique is *stockless purchasing*. Under this method, a buyer selects one or more restaurant supply houses who, in exchange for certain volume guarantees over a fixed period of time, are asked to stock and guarantee the price of the inventory required by the operation and to ship all orders received from the individual operating locations.

This purchasing arrangement has advantages for both buyer and seller. For the buyer, it offers a known service program wherein each operating unit can obtain all the materials required without the need for individual purchase negotiations every time. He also obtains his materials at a price which is generally far superior to that which could be obtained if competitive bidding took place each time he had a need for merchandise. What is of even more importance to the buyer is the fact that the supply house participating in this program is maintaining the buyer's inventory for him at no charge, and is guaranteeing the execution of a prenegotiated shipping schedule each time an order is received from one of the operating locations. The buyer knows what his costs will be for each item over a predetermined period of time, thus locking in another important segment of his profit plan for the period covered by the agreement.

At the present time, a number of the major restaurant chains in the United States are engaged in some form of stockless purchasing program for at least a portion of their tabletop requirements. The only drawback to this type of program is the relatively large annual expenditure for tabletop items on the part of the operator necessary to establish it. The individual restaurant operation or the small chain expending less than $5,000 per year for tabletop items might find it difficult to locate a restaurant supply house willing to participate in this type of program. However, if a buyer were able to arrange to have his tabletop requirements set up in such a way as to only use items that are normally carried in the stock of the typical supply house, a program of this type might be established on a much smaller requirements basis.

The advantages to the vendor in establishing a stockless purchasing program for a food service operation stem mainly from the added predictability and increased volume which such a program provides for his business. If the vendor knows specifically how many items a given chain will require over a known period of time and has received a commitment from that chain to purchase that item, he is guaranteed a certain amount of business from that operation and can concentrate his energies on developing business from other customers. If the buyer recognizes the benefits that will accrue to the vendor and brings them to the vendor's attention during the course of his price and terms negotiations, he can frequently convert this knowledge into lower prices or improved service.

Other Considerations

Although the buyer is not normally charged with the responsibility of designing the tabletop arrangement for a food service establishment, he should insure that the products selected are affordable, available in adequate supply, and durable. Many a restaurant operation has settled on a particular design of china or flatware only to find that its availability is strictly limited; its price is substantially above that for similar materials, it tends to chip or scratch easily, or its appeal to souvenir hunters requires that it be replenished constantly.

Of course, there are circumstances in which the restaurant deliberately designs an item with an advertising message on it for its customers to take home as a souvenir of their dining experience. If this is the case with a particular ash tray or cocktail glass, the replenishment cost of the item should be charged to advertising or local promotion, rather than to the tabletop account. However, there are many other situations in which the operator finds certain pieces of his tabletop ensemble disappearing when he least expects it. When this happens, the buyer may have to get together with other operating personnel in the organization to examine alternate designs or structures for the tabletop ensemble and to come up with a design package that will be less attractive to the souvenir hunter. He might also suggest more emphasis on training service personnel to remove items that are attractive as souvenirs when not actually in use.

Over the past five years, the average cost increases for the commonly defined tabletop items has exceeded 10% per annum. There is every indication that these annual price advances will continue for at least the next five years. This means that by 1980, a tabletop will cost one hundred percent more than its counterpart of 1970. With the restaurant operator facing constantly increasing costs for food and labor, to say nothing of taxes and utilities, all possible steps must be taken to reduce the cost of the tabletop, which is a fixed and growing expense of running a food service operation.

OPERATING SUPPLIES

When we talk about operating supplies for the food service industry, we are describing those nonfood items which do not appear on the tabletop. This includes such items as pots, pans, kitchen implements such as knives, stirring spoons, gravy ladles, etc., preparation equipment such as large mixing containers and refrigerator storage containers, cleaning equipment of all types, and cleaning compounds. Specifically excluded from this group are items that are purchased on a one-time basis such as dishwashing machines or deep fat fryers. These items are capital expense items and will be treated separately in a following chapter.

As in the case of tabletop items, operating supplies frequently fall into that unfortunate category of forgotten items which are purchased more as a nuisance factor than as a true opportunity for the food service operation to conserve funds and reduce costs. The small operator should approach the purchase of operating supplies in much the same fashion that he negotiates for tabletop items. This means selecting a major supplier who fully understands his requirements and can supply the items he needs on a fixed price, guaranteed delivery basis.

Cleaning Supplies

A special word is in order about the purchase of cleaning supplies such as soaps, stain removers, and water softeners. With these particular items, usage rate is as important as price when determining which supplier is offering the most attractive proposal. A lower priced dishwashing compound may in fact be used up much more quickly than a higher priced competitive product.

The knowledgeable buyer will ask his cleaning supplies vendor to provide trial quantities of the different compounds he is considering before he reaches any final decision. He should then use these trial quantities in carefully monitored evaluation tests to develop a better perspective on the price/rate of usage factors for each product.

If he takes the time to do this with each of his cleaning supplies, he will be in a better position to assure himself that he is, in fact, getting the best value, not only in terms of price, but also in terms of performance.

The buyer for the chain operation may take the cleaning supplies procurement program one step further by establishing long-term procurement and distribution arrangements to further improve his purchase price on cleaning compounds. Although the major detergent companies have established elaborate distribution networks throughout the United States, they are willing to consider customer distribution systems if the annual volume purchased by the customer is large enough. This affords the buyer the opportunity of buying these products in bulk and then distributing them to his units with other food products and supplies.

Another consideration in the purchase of cleaning supplies is the service that the vendor renders to the operator's cleaning equipment. This primarily concerns the dish machine and the water softening equipment in an operation. Most reputable firms supplying cleaning compounds to the food service industry provide machine service 24 hours a day. While the buyer may not require these services very often, it is important that he negotiate them into his procurement contract, so that if and when they are necessary, they will be available without delay. A broken dishwashing machine can bring a high volume food service operation to a grinding halt. If the buyer has taken the time to negotiate a service arrangement into his procurement contract for cleaning compounds, the danger of a malfunctioning dish machine creating a major interruption in the kitchen will be minimized. Many buyers find out about the seriousness of this problem only by bitter experience. If the buyer takes precautions early, he will be better able to avoid these unpleasant situations.

As a final wrap-up on the purchase of tabletop items and operating supplies for either the small restaurant operation or the major food service chain, the following points should be noted:

- Choose your supplier carefully, and only after making sure that he understands precisely what your requirements are regarding not only inventory to be kept available, but also delivery and credit arrangements.
- Develop a forecast of long-term requirements so that you may

improve your purchasing leverage with your supplier by offering him an extended contract.

- Carefully monitor your expenditures for tabletop items and operating supplies to be sure that together they do not exceed 3–4% of your operation's gross sales. If they do, you have a problem which requires immediate attention.

Chapter 9 Questions

1. Why is it particularly important that expense categories for table-top items and operating supplies be carefully monitored?

2. What is meant by *stockless purchasing?*

3. Describe how you would set up a stockless purchasing program for (1) a single unit operation, and (2) a 100-unit chain?

4. How can a buyer best develop competition among potential vendors of operating supplies?

5. Discuss how yield and service can become as important as price in the purchase of cleaning compounds.

10

Equipment Programs in the Food Service Industry

DISPENSING EQUIPMENT

One of the programs peculiar to the food service industry involves dispensing equipment offered by suppliers to facilitate the service of their products. This includes dishwashing machines and water softeners with automatic compound dispensing capability, instant tea machines, instant hot chocolate machines, a wide variety of equipment that dispenses coffee, carbonated beverages, draft beer, orange juice and other fruit beverages, and even freezers that dispense ice cream.

One might wonder how all these programs can exist when the cost of this machinery is an obvious burden on the vendor who supplies it. Lest we concern ourselves too much with the vendor's profit margin, let me assure you that no vendor of any product that requires dispensing equipment ever lost money providing that equipment to his customer as a part of his supply package.

The large, reputable suppliers explain that the cost of their equipment is built into the cost of the product being dispensed from it. For example, if you were to approach a large coffee roaster and ask for two prices, one reflecting so called "free" equipment to be placed in your unit, and the other a net price based on the cost of the coffee alone, you would find a price differential ranging from six to fourteen cents per pound (the lower price reflecting the sale of the coffee alone). Equipment placed in the unit by the manufacturer obviously serves a very important purpose for the user. But neither the user nor the buyer who procures equipment and the dispensed products should forget that this equipment is not free. You are paying for it in the price of the product which will be dispensed through it.

There are several important considerations the buyer should evaluate before deciding whether to arrange for such a program. First and probably foremost is the financial condition of the food service operation. If the company is stable and has adequate financial resources to buy its own equipment, there is probably little justification for taking the equipment and paying a surcharge on every pound or gallon of product dispensed through that equipment. If, however, it is a new organization just getting started which has severe capital demands up front, it might make sense to accept this equipment and pay the surcharge until such time as the organization has sufficient liquidity to purchase the equipment outright.

A simple analysis of the financial alternatives will usually indicate which course is desirable. For example, let us consider a piece of coffee brewing equipment with a theoretical cost of $800.00. The coffee supplier is perfectly willing to place the piece of equipment in the unit and charge an override of 10¢ per pound as an offset against the cost of the equipment. This may seem very attractive to the buyer, but he should do a quick calculation to determine how long it will take to consume 8,000 pounds of coffee, or the price of a new machine. (8,000 pounds times 10¢ per pound equals $800.00—the full cost of a brand new piece of equipment.)

If his operation consumes 100 pounds of coffee per week, this means he will be paying a surcharge of $520.00 per year for the use of the "free" equipment. With a life expectancy of some five to seven years, the buyer can expect to pay the cost of the equipment three to four times over. If, however, his coffee consumption was only 30 pounds per week, the same calculation would indicate that it would take five to six years at 10¢ per pound before the buyer would have accumulated the total cost of the piece of equipment.

It is difficult to generalize about which course of action is best in each particular situation. To determine which is best for his individual firm, the buyer should take his usage pattern and calculate the total surcharge payment he will be required to pay on an annual basis. He can then compare this figure with the cost of the equipment and make his decision regarding participation in the supplier's equipment program.

Another alternative not always available to the smaller operator is a surcharge payment program on equipment in which ownership of the equipment reverts to the buyer at a specific point when a fixed amount of funds has been accumulated in the form of surcharge payments. Let's say that a major chain operation with 300 outlets decides to take an equipment program from a purveyor of frozen orange juice concentrate with the understanding that after paying $300 in surcharge payments (at a surcharge of fifty cents per case he must have used a total of 600 cases per machine), ownership of the machine reverts to the buyer. In a situation of this type (and especially in high volume locations) the consumption of the frozen orange juice concentrate through the machine is rapid enough to result in a full payback of the vendor's expense in supplying the machine well before the useful life of the machine has ended. Naturally, the supplier would prefer to have a fifty-cent per case payment continue indefinitely. However, the astute buyer can utilize the substantial leverage generated in a large food service organization to reach an agreement with the supplier for transfer of machine ownership after payment of a specific surcharge amount.

Another word of caution: Such a program frequently inhibits or actually restricts the flexibility of the buyer in changing suppliers for a fixed period of time after the equipment has been installed. Many suppliers ask that a buyer sign an agreement that if the equipment is placed in his operation, the buyer must continue to purchase the product from that supplier for a specific period of time. I have seen agreements of this kind specifying periods of time of up to three years in duration.

The reasoning for such agreements is fairly simple. The vendor, in supplying the equipment, wants to be assured that his product will be used for a relatively long period of time so that the buyer will be paying total surcharges sufficient to allow the vendor to amortize the cost of the machine. If this does not happen, the vendor may very well be left with a piece of used equipment (all equipment is used one day after it has been placed in service) which he will find very difficult to place in a new account. Hence, the buyer must recognize the vendor's right to require a long-term commitment in exchange for the placement of equipment, and he must take this fact into account in making his decision regarding participation in an equipment program.

SOME ADVANTAGES TO EQUIPMENT PROGRAMS

In the last few years a whole new array of equipment items for the food service industry has come to the market. We now have our choice of such exotic machines as instant French fry extrusion devices, machines that will roll and bake a crepe in one operation, espresso machines, cold water glass washing equipment, automatic liquor dispensing devices, etc., etc. There is no doubt that the continuing advancements in machine technology in the food service industry will result in an ever-growing array of this type of equipment. In many cases it is to the vendor's advantage to include the machine as a part of his sales package. The buyer should realize that while under certain conditions, an equipment program is very much in his best interest, there are numerous other times when he should avoid it if at all possible.

An equipment program might be of specific and quite positive value to the buyer when some piece of equipment has just been brought to market and its utility or operational value has still not been fully tested. The buyer should be very wary lest he purchase a piece of equipment which is either not fully capable of doing the job that it was intended to do or is quickly rendered obsolete by a new development in the market. An excellent example of this risk occurred in the computer industry during the late 1950's when customers who purchased computers more often than not found them obsolete long before their useful life had expired. Although there has not been a heavy incidence of this trend in the food service industry, substantial advances in machine technology in the last few years have created a definite possibility of obsolescence. Once a machine has been tested under actual operating conditions for several years, it is generally safe for the buyer to consider making an investment in it.

GUIDELINES TO FOLLOW

There are so many different equipment programs available to the food service industry, with various features that change so frequently, that an attempt to describe each one of them in detail would serve no purpose.

However, here are a few general guidelines that any buyer, regardless of the size of his food service operation, should consider before participating in an equipment program.

1. Always perform a consumption/surcharge analysis for each piece of equipment that you are thinking of accepting from a vendor. This means comparing the amount of surcharge you expect to pay during the life of the equipment agreement with the actual cost of the equipment if you were to purchase it outright. Remember that when you participate in an equipment program, you lose the advantages of depreciation which would accrue to you if the equipment were to be purchased outright. This loss in depreciation should be reviewed with the financial people in your organization, who should be given a full opportunity to assess its impact on the overall cash flow of the company. While the buyer may be the one to recommend which alternative he suggests—outright equipment purchase or participation in a vendor's equipment program—he should never presume to make a decision as to the importance of depreciation to his company's cash flow. In the larger food service operations, particularly, the depreciation factor can have a substantial impact on cash flow.
2. Always examine the contract covering the equipment agreement very carefully. If possible, have an attorney evaluate the contract and the burdens it places on the buyer's organization. Remember that these contracts are legally binding on the buyer and his company.
3. Under certain circumstances it may be advantageous to ask the vendor if, rather than placing new equipment in his location, the vendor has used equipment which he will place in the operation for a shorter period of time. If the vendor has been faced with other customers who discontinued their equipment programs, he may be very interested in exploring this type of special arrangement, since it gives him an opportunity to place used equipment (which is generally difficult to place) and still receive a surcharge on his product in return. Naturally, the buyer who is able to negotiate this type of agreement with the vendor should insist on a significantly shorter period of time during which the agreement will endure, and should even be able to negotiate a smaller per unit surcharge payment.

4. Beware of the vendor who refuses to identify the specific per unit surcharge which is being levied for the use of the equipment. Any vendor's representative who insists that the equipment is "free" is not being totally open with you and should therefore be treated with great caution.
5. Always try to negotiate an agreement with the vendor such that after a specific amount of surcharge monies have been paid, ownership of the piece of equipment will revert to you.
6. The buyer should insist that any program he enters into provide that the supplier of the equipment bear 100% of the responsibility for service and repairs. Although many equipment programs contain this clause as a matter of course, you should make sure that this stipulation is a written part of the agreement. Do not waive this stipulation under any circumstances.

In addition to a provision for vendor responsibility, the agreement should also state within what period of time service must be provided. A broken coffee urn in a restaurant that does not have standby equipment can bring the entire operation to a halt. Most vendors who offer equipment programs back them up with 24-hour service coverage. The buyer should include in his negotiations an agreement as to the maximum amount of time allowed before the supplier must respond to a service call. This may range from six hours up to 24 hours, depending upon the particular item being covered in the service agreement. Whatever the arrangement, it is essential that some stipulation of this type be formally included in the agreement.

Chapter 10 Questions

1. What questions should the buyer ask himself when evaluating the alternatives of equipment purchase vs. participation in a supplier's equipment program?

2. Describe the type of financial analysis which the buyer should conduct before making the purchase vs. equipment program decision.

3. Why is it important to have a prior agreement with the vendor as to the point at which the equipment surcharge will cease to be added to the product cost?

4. What are the primary advantages and disadvantages of participating in an equipment program?

5. How can participation in an equipment program restrict a buyer's flexibility?

11

The Purchase of Capital Items

CAPITAL EQUIPMENT

In the previous chapter we considered the advantages and disadvantages of equipment programs offered by vendors. Let us now consider in more detail the specific purchasing considerations which the food service operator should evaluate as he purchases capital equipment.

For purposes of this discussion, *capital equipment* shall be defined as any piece of equipment required for the food service operation which has a purchase price of $500 or more. Included in this category are a broad spectrum of items ranging from tables and chairs to kitchen equipment such as deep fat fryers, convection ovens, refrigeration equipment, preparation tables, and warewashing machines. Additionally, items such as heating, ventilating, and air-conditioning equipment, cash registers, security devices, music systems, vending equipment, and even decorative accessories such as lighting fixtures and wall hangings might fall into this category.

The one thing that all of these items have in common is their expense. They are not items that are purchased on a repetitive basis. As a result, the buyer must be particularly careful to do a thorough research job prior to their purchase. It is perfectly natural for a buyer or food service operator to look on the purchase of a warewashing machine or deep fat fryer as a necessary ingredient for his operation and to forget that the opportunity for competitive bidding and price negotiation exists as much for these items as it does for some of his major foodstuff ingredients. As in all buying activity, knowing what you want and then carefully testing the market place to obtain at least three competitive bids is probably the best guarantee of getting the best buy each time.

When purchasing capital equipment, the buyer should have a written specification outlining in detail exactly what piece of equipment he is looking for and what he expects it to do. He should give this specification to all potential suppliers, along with the request for their evaluation of it based on their experience selling similar pieces of equipment to other food service operators. There is nothing wrong with the buyer's putting this type of burden on the vendor and requiring him to provide some kind of evaluative response to the specification.

Frequently the vendor will be in a position where his own experience can be of invaluable assistance. Although he may welcome an opportunity to provide comments on a particular equipment specification, he may nevertheless hesitate unless asked for fear of alienating a buyer who may feel that a vendor who volunteers such constructive criticism is out of order. There is no disgrace in asking a vendor for his comments and opinions. In most cases the vendor has had substantially more experience with the particular piece of equipment than the buyer and is therefore in a far stronger position to provide helpful guidelines and insight to the buyer.

Unlike the purchase of meat, poultry, or vegetables, which are repeated weekly and often daily, the purchase of a deep fat fryer or a dish washing machine is a long-term investment in which there is little room for mistaken purchases.

VENDOR SELECTION

The process of vendor selection can follow a number of different forms, depending upon the size of the operation and the buyer's familiarity with the local market. In addition to the time-tested technique of starting with the yellow pages, another excellent means of reference for the buyer who is unfamiliar with vendors in a particular area is to seek references from his associates in other food service operations. The actual experience of these other buyers—either positive or negative—can be of great assistance in eliminating the time that might otherwise be spent with vendors who are either unqualified or unable to provide the service desired.

Once a list of vendors has been developed (at least three potential sources for each piece of capital equipment), the buyer should contact these suppliers for a preliminary interview to discuss his specific needs. There is no point in scheduling a meeting of this type unless the buyer is fully equipped with specifications detailing the requirements of each item he wishes to purchase.

The initial meeting should be a purely exploratory session, wherein the buyer learns about the vendor and the vendor understands the specifications on the equipment, and where both are given an opportunity to ask questions. Naturally, if the buyer is doing business with a company with whom he has had previous experience, these preliminary sessions will not be necessary, since the buyer has presumably established a working relationship with vendors who have submitted acceptable bids and service in the past. He is thus able to proceed directly to the second step of the capital equipment procurement process—the solicitation of sealed competitive bids. (Of course the buyer should always keep the door open for new suppliers wishing to become first-time bidders.)

Although the small food service operator may feel that this is applicable only to the major chain operations, quite the contrary is true. The major chain, with many more dollars to be spent, will obviously enter into a much more detailed development and evaluation of competitive bids. However, the individual operator or the small multi-unit chain must recognize that *as a percentage of total sales,* their expenditures for capital equipment are every bit as significant as those of the major chain, and as such, it will pay to approach capital equipment procurement in a careful and detailed fashion.

BIDDING

Along with the specifications, the buyer should forward to each vendor a brief written description of the bidding procedures which the buyer will follow. He should make absolutely certain that this description specifies clearly the form in which the bid should be submitted and the date by which it must be in. He should also indicate on the form that bids are being requested from a number of different purveyors, that the bids will be opened at a specific time and place, and that he reserves the right to reject any bid deemed unacceptable for any reason. This qualification in all competitive bidding procedures is necessary to protect the buyer from a "low ball" bid submitted by an obviously unqualified supplier, or from a low bid submitted by a vendor with whom the buyer has had previous unsatisfactory experience.

Once the bids have been received and opened, there is little more for the buyer to do than to award the contract to the lowest bidder. However, handling the sealed bids as submitted by the prospective suppliers places a very deep responsibility on the buyer not to abuse or in any way violate the confidentiality of these bids. A public bid-opening ceremony as followed by most municipal organizations is an excellent way to demonstrate to all concerned that the confidentiality of the sealed bids has been maintained. A further way of assuring this confidentiality is to request a third party, preferably an officer of the food service organization other than the buyer, to actually open the sealed bids.

Equipment Installation

There are two other areas which the buyer should remember in preparing his request for quotations on capital equipment. First, he should be sure that the vendor understands that his bid should include all costs for equipment installation. The buyer should clearly specify that he is buying a piece of equipment on an installed basis, rather than F.O.B. the vendor's warehouse or F.O.B. his point of use. Frequently a vendor will recommend that the buyer accept a quotation on an F.O.B. destination basis, which simply means that the box or crate containing the piece of equipment is delivered to the user's door. Installation responsibility then becomes the buyer's, and in the great majority of cases, these installation costs will be greater than the vendor's. Most buyers who have had experience in the procurement of capital equipment have learned from bitter experience that where installation is required, they should include it in the basic cost of the equipment at the time bids are received.

PRODUCT WARRANTY AND SERVICE RESPONSIBILITY

The other important area for the buyer to consider is the question of product warranty and service responsibility during the warranty period. Obviously, the longer the warranty, the more protection the buyer has against the possible malfunction of the item. A warranty alone, however, will not solve his problem if a machine breaks down. It is one thing to have a sound product warranty and quite another to obtain the service required to correct the malfunction. The buyer should be especially careful to establish clearly and unequivocably the vendor's responsibility for providing service under any warranty clause. If the vendor is unwilling to do this, the buyer should immediately eliminate him from consideration as a potential source of supply.

FINANCIAL CONTROLS

Although not a primary responsibility of either the purchasing department or the capital equipment buyer, financial controls which must exist on all capital items are sufficiently important so that the purchasing area should be cognizant of them. Very simply, these controls include proper forecasting of capital equipment requirements, budgeting for the requirements as forecast, identification and periodic inventorying of all capital equipment items once they have been purchased, establishment of a depreciation schedule designed to amortize the cost of the particular piece of equipment over its useful life, and a program for disposal of equipment that has become obsolete, either because it is no longer useful or because of general deterioration.

Forecasting

Forecasting of capital equipment requirements is very important to protect the operation against unpleasant surprises, such as unanticipated expenditures of several thousand dollars for a piece of equipment that no one expected to purchase. The operations executive responsible for a particular operation should be charged with the responsibility of forecasting his capital equipment requirements at least twelve months in advance. In those operations of sufficient size to be able to forecast for longer periods of time, so much the better. If such forecasting is not done in your operation, the buyer should take steps to put such a procedure into effect. While the buyer may not be in a position to provide the forecast, he should certainly be able to request it if need be.

The forecasting procedure should include an examination of the current condition of all capital items presently on the books and an estimate of their remaining useful life. It should also include a review of repair records on each piece of equipment to show how much money is being spent to repair existing equipment. This information can then be weighed against the cost of new equpiment when decisions about replacing the equipment before it has been fully depreciated come up. If a particular piece of equipment turns out to be a true lemon, requiring many more maintenance and service expenditures than had been expected, the buyer's first action should be to notify the manufacturer and try to obtain some relief. If this is not available, he should then consider an early replacement of the unit.

I have had personal experience with certain pieces of refrigeration equipment that have continuous compressor problems. Although these instances are infrequent, they can be very annoying and extremely costly. In situations like this it pays to contact the supplier, explain the problem to him, and request either a product replacement or a pro rata adjustment of the original purchase price to reflect the inordinate maintenance and service expense which has been necessary. This could take the form of a price adjustment on an early replacement or the vendor's assuming the expense of future service calls. Naturally, suppliers will react differently to such requests, depending upon their relationship with the customer, the amount of volume they are doing with him in a given period of time, and their past experience with this particular piece of machinery. If the buyer is unable to achieve satisfaction from his supplier, he should then consider recommending an early replacement of the unit.

Budget Provisions

Once the capital equipment forecast has been completed and reviewed with the purchasing department, the next step is the appropriate provision in the upcoming budget for the capital expenditure. This budget should take into account the useful life of each piece of equipment, so that a depreciation schedule can be established and plugged into future financial plans. Depreciation is nothing more than taking the total cost of the piece of equipment and dividing that cost by the useful life of the item. The useful life may be expressed in either years or months, so the depreciation charge per accounting period may be expressed on a similar basis. If the projection of useful life has been accurate and the depreciation schedule followed, at the end of the estimated useful life, the full value of the unit should be written off. Hence it can be said to have a zero book value.

Proper Identification and Inventorying

Another important control device to be used in connection with capital equipment is proper identification and periodic inventorying of the item. As big as pieces of capital equipment usually are, they still have a way of disappearing if they are not properly identified and inventoried. It is one thing for a food service operation to lose a pound of bacon or a crate of lettuce. It is quite another, however, to have an expensive slicing machine or a microwave oven disappear from the premises.

Identification is usually obtained by affixing a company serial number to the unit. While this may not always help to locate a missing item, it can be of psychological value in deterring an employee who may be considering the theft of the item. Inventorying, on the other hand, helps determine the status of your equipment. It should include a brief notation as to the current condition of the piece of equipment, and should be taken on a quarterly basis. If this is done properly, it should keep an operation up-to-date on each piece of equipment and its condition.

BUYING USED EQUIPMENT

A final consideration regarding the purchase of capital equipment is the possibility of occasionally purchasing used rather than new merchandise. This would be advantageous for seasonal operations in which new equipment often goes unused for a significant portion of the year, for food service operations without a long-term contract that assures its continued functioning, and for buyers who can purchase slightly used equipment at significant discounts. If the capital equipment buyer encounters situations like this, he should give careful thought to the advantages of buying the used equipment.

Obviously, the most significant advantage is the cost reduction compared with the purchase of new equipment. As anyone who has ever attended an auction of used food service equipment knows, it is customary for such equipment to sell at anywhere from fifteen to thirty percent of the cost of the original equipment. Frequently, the equipment in these auctions is almost new and will perform quite satisfactorily for a long period of time. There is nothing wrong with purchasing used equipment as long as either a bona fide price value relationship can be identified or some other extenuating circumstance warrants its purchase.

Chapter 11 Questions

1. Why are capital items often not subjected to the same type of competitive bidding procurement as are the foodstuffs consumed in a food service operation?

2. What should be included in the product specifications used by the buyer in soliciting competitive bids on capital equipment?

3. Discuss how failure to include precise instructions as to freight charges and installation costs can negate the competitive bidding process on capital items.

4. How should product warranty and service responsibilities be handled in the purchase of capital equipment?

5. When might it make sense for the buyer to consider the purchase of used equipment?

12

Purchasing Procedures and Controls

OVERVIEW

If you were to go to a library to research business books relating specifically to the purchasing profession, you would find that more pages are devoted to the subject of purchasing procedures and controls than to any other single area of the purchasing spectrum. In this chapter I will attempt to distill the most important aspects of these numerous writings and focus on those specific applications which are most effective in the food service industry. Since the individual food service operation is essentially a microcosm of the giant chain, these aspects and applications apply to both equally.

Sometimes procedures and controls in any field are looked upon as a constant nuisance, irritation, and waste of time. At other times, when they have prevented a serious business problem, they may be praised as the backbone of the particular business. Such is also the case with the procedures and controls which are used in all aspects of purchasing for the food service industry. However, be they nuisance or backbone, by concentrating on the fundamentals, you will be more likely to contribute to a more efficient and successful operation.

Historically, the purchasing procedural cycle has included requisitions, purchase orders, shipping instructions (specific directions to the supplier about the individual delivery), receiving reports, quality control inspection reports, yield analyses, waste control reports, purchasing history records, supplier performance reports, projections of future needs, price forecasting, and many more. To say that each of these areas is essential to every food service purchasing function is nonsense. However, the good buyer should be aware of each of these procedures and control techniques whether he uses them or not, so he can adapt each of them to his own particular operation.

Thus in a major food service operation having its own commissary consuming large weekly quantities of meat, poultry, flour, vegetable oil and seafood, a written requisition from production to purchasing is an absolute necessity. However, in the smaller restaurant operation a standing weekly order with the produce supplier or the dairy vendor might not require a written requisition at all from anyone in order to trigger it each week. The important thing for the buyer to remember is that at all times he should have sufficient purchasing procedures and controls to adequately cover his particular operation, and should maintain enough flexibility to modify each of these control points to meet the needs of his particular operation.

THE PURCHASING REQUISITION

The buyer should look on this document as the action that starts the purchasing cycle. A requisition is simply a request of some kind to order an item. It may take the form of a written request, a verbal conversation, a phone call, or simply a copy of last week's order with the notation, "Please reorder." The individual buyer must determine to what extent he needs a formalized requisition, realizing at all times that his job is to avoid purchasing all unnecessary materials, unless it involves an opportunity buy.

As a general rule, there is a direct correlation between the size of the restaurant operation and the degree to which its requisition system should be formalized. However, a small operation, even a one-unit business, can follow the essential guidelines of a requisition system even without preprinted requisition forms covering each purchase. In effect, establishing some kind of requisition system recognizes the need for a specific request (requisition) to trigger the purchasing cycle.

In the large organization the requisition can serve a very important secondary purpose in addition to initiating the purchasing cycle. It is also a permanent record of who initiated the request for the purchase, on what date, for what delivery, and for what quantity and quality. As is frequently the case in larger food service organizations, poor internal communications and/or personnel turnover can result in situations where management asks the purchasing department questions concerning the rationale for a particular purchase. This is especially true when a firm finds itself with a substantial excess inventory at a time when the market price is dropping sharply. At that time an accusing finger is frequently pointed at the buyer with a demand for an explanation as to, "How did you ever get us in this position?" At a time like that, the buyer must be able to turn to his file and produce a requisition showing that Mr. X in the Manufacturing Department or Miss Y in the Cafeteria requested this amount of product on such-and-such a date. I have seen this type of situation develop so many times in my purchasing career that I cannot stress strongly enough this secondary value of the written requisition.

THE PURCHASE ORDER

After the buyer receives the requisition, it is his task to implement it by obtaining the best possible price, quality, and delivery for the material requested on the requisition. The control document that covers this part of the purchasing cycle is the *purchase order*. This is a legal contract between buyer and seller stating the terms on which the purchase is to be consummated. Although requisitions do not necessarily need to be put in writing, purchase orders must always be written. Even in the smallest organization the purchase order should be in writing, not only to guard against misunderstanding on the part of the supplier, but also as justification for the payment of invoices, which will shortly follow the delivery of the merchandise.

The purchase order should state very specifically the quantity and quality of merchandise desired, the price which has been agreed upon for the merchandise, the time and place of delivery, the method of packaging, and any other terms and conditions which the buyer feels are necessary. Each purchase order should be separately numbered to serve as a further control and reference point for the payment of invoices and for whatever purchasing records are maintained.

A great deal of wasted time and effort goes into the typing of purchase orders, not only in the food service industry but in business in general. I have experimented with the handwritten purchase order with great success and use it in all purchasing situations except for high value, long-term contracts. The advantages of the handwritten purchase order fall into two distinct categories. First is the obvious saving in clerical time and expense, which is considerably more than most people suspect. (An analysis of your own buying office might surprise you.)

A very important second advantage of handwritten purchase orders is the improvement in accuracy which results from the buyer's completing the purchase order at the very moment when he and the seller agree on the transaction. The document can be completed and signed by the buyer when the transaction is finalized. With a typewritten purchase order, the possibility of misinterpretation by the typist exists, resulting in the preparation of an incorrect purchase order. The document must then be retyped and returned to the buyer for his signature prior to being forwarded to the vendor. These extra steps and possible areas of confusion and error are totally eliminated when the buyer utilizes the handwritten purchase order.

With the recent applications of computer technology to the purchasing profession, many companies are already preparing their purchase orders on a computer. Obviously, if your organization has reached this level of sophistication, you need not consider handwritten purchase orders, since a computer is handling that function for the buying department. However, since the vast majority of food service organizations have not yet reached this point, the handwritten purchase order will be around for a long time to come and is still the most economical, efficient, and precise form for most firms.

THE SHIPPING INSTRUCTION

This is the document which activates individual shipments against large or blanket purchase orders. There are many times in any food service organization when a long-term purchase agreement is consummated. This may range from an individual operator who makes an agreement with his local dairy supplier for a fixed price on milk for a period of sixty days, to the large chain that enters into a national contract covering all its units for a one-year supply of ketchup or pickles. In each case specific deliveries against this master purchase order must be triggered by a separate document, the shipping instruction.

The shipping instruction serves as a confirmation of instructions forwarded from the buyer to the seller relating to a specific delivery of merchandise. It can be very simple in form and context, and, unless there are unusual circumstances requiring it, should be handwritten. It should contain the purchase order number against which the shipment is being made, and should also be individually numbered for purposes of record keeping and for a historical reconstruction of all shipments against a given purchase contract.

THE RECEIVING REPORT

Another important purchasing document not always recognized within the purchasing profession is the receiving report. This is nothing more than an internal acknowledgment of receipt of the merchandise covered in the earlier requisition, purchase order, and shipping instruction. This document should be prepared by the person actually receiving the merchandise from the vendor. In a smaller operation it may be one of the kitchen employees, the chef, or the manager of the operation. The larger food service establishments often have a specific receiving department established expressly for the purpose of checking all incoming merchandise.

In either case the receiving report should indicate the quantity and condition of the merchandise received. If there are any variances from the requirements as stated on the purchase order, these should be clearly noted on the receiving report. If he finds either a shortage of product or a variation in the quality requested, the person completing the receiving report should make sure that the individual making the delivery signs the report and acknowledges the deficiency in the delivery. The person completing the report should also sign and date it.

As in the case of other purchasing control documents, the receiving report should be no more complicated than necessary. In a small food service operation it may simply be a notation entered on the bill of lading (documents which accompany a shipment) or the invoice, stating briefly the condition of the shipment. In the larger operation, especially one involved with manufacturing, copies of the receiving report should be forwarded to the quality control department, the purchasing department, and the accounting area.

The quality control department needs a copy of the receiving report so they are notified that a shipment has been received and they have an inspection chore to perform: They must arrange to have the merchandise inspected for compliance with company specifications. Ideally this inspection should take place at the time the merchandise is delivered. Many larger food service organizations establish a system whereby the receiving report is prepared by the individual responsible for quality control inspection. However, such coordination is not always possible, even in a large organization, since merchandise arrives during nonbusiness hours.

The purchasing department needs the copy of the receiving report to close their file on the shipping instruction which has been issued against a specific purchase order, and to keep advised of any discrepancy between the merchandise ordered and delivered.

The accounting department uses the receiving report as a match against the purchase order and the vendor's invoice prior to preparing payment for the merchandise. By comparing the purchase order, the receiving report, and the vendor's invoice, the accounting department has a three-way check prior to payment of the invoice. If there are any discrepancies between the quantity and quality listed on any of these documents, they must be resolved before a payment goes out.

QUALITY CONTROL

The quality control inspection, while not a direct function of the purchasing department, is an important control in the overall purchasing cycle. If it does not occur, it can reduce the effectiveness of purchasing controls. One moderate sized fast food operation I know took great pride in a company-wide purchase agreement with a large regional meat packing house. The agreement, which covered delivery of hamburger to all units, called for hamburger with a fat content not to exceed 20%. However, the company had no provision for testing the fat content of individual deliveries to its units. Over a period of time, the meat supplier either deliberately or inadvertently allowed the fat content to rise to approximately 24%. The chain, however, was completely unaware of this change in product quality because of its lack of quality control testing.

The matter came to light in an unfortunate way. After the chain ran newspaper ads advertising that its hamburger contained no more than 20% fat, a local consumer protection agency went to one of the units, picked up samples, and had them analyzed in an outside laboratory. Much to the chagrin of the management of the operation, the samples all showed fat content in excess of 24%. The resulting adverse publicity certainly did not help this operation.

While this particular case may seem extreme to some, it nevertheless shows what can happen when some sort of quality evaluation on incoming materials is not performed. In a small operation, this evaluation may simply involve the owner or chef conducting periodic inspections of individual shipments from every vendor. For the larger operation that has its own separate quality control department, it will involve an analysis of each and every delivery of merchandise to its locations. The principle is the same; it is simply the application that will differ, depending on the operation.

When a quality control analysis indicates any discrepancy between the product specified on the purchase order and the product actually received, the purchasing department should be notified immediately. The purchasing department must then assume the responsibility of communicating to the vendor any dissatisfaction with the product. Neither the quality control department nor any other individual in the company should assume this responsibility unless he does so under the auspices of the purchasing department. Any buyer who becomes aware of communication of this type between other representatives of his firm and a vendor's organization should take immediate steps to eliminate it.

I stress this point because it has been my experience that such communication tends to weaken the effectiveness of the buyer in his future contact with the vendor. If the vendor is contacted by non-purchasing people, he will naturally concentrate his efforts on appeasing the complaining party, which may not be a purchasing person. Since the buyer is unaware of the communication between the vendor and the other individual, and since he cannot therefore take it into account in negotiating subsequent orders, his effectiveness gradually erodes. If, however, the purchasing department knows of discrepancies, the buyer can then use this information either to negotiate an improved arrangement with the vendor or to make a decision about terminating his relationship with that particular firm.

In summary, the strength and effectiveness which a buyer can develop depends to some extent on the degree of communication between the supplier and the purchasing department. I am not suggesting that from time to time the buyer will not want to involve other members of his organization in discussion with his suppliers. However, he and no one else should be the judge of when this contact is appropriate.

YIELD ANALYSES AND WASTE REPORTS

As an extension of quality control inspection, the particular food service operation may also wish to utilize two other techniques that helps to insure maximum value. These are yield analyses and waste control reports. Yield analysis is the process of comparing the net output of comparable products received from different suppliers. For example, three different bacon suppliers who each supply seemingly identical products to a food service chain may differ substantially in product output once the bacon has been cooked. A simple yield analysis involves taking one pound of each supplier's product, cooking it, and then weighing it again to determine which of the three suppliers is producing the best value for the dollar expended. There are numerous applications of yield analysis in the food service industry, the result of which can help any buyer to improve the efficiency of his buying job.

Another technique which is a natural extension of the yield analysis is a waste control report. This analysis keeps track of all waste in the kitchen and identifies it by product and by supplier. If a given item shows an inordinately high degree of waste, then the buyer should question the supplier of that product. Since the buyer is not normally on the scene when the product is being consumed, the only way that he will learn of waste problems is through a waste control report. There is no set form for such analysis. Each organization usually structures its own form based on its own particular needs. (See Figure 20.)

Frequently information provided by these two control techniques justifies paying a higher price to a particular supplier because of better yield and/or less waste from that vendor's product. The yield analysis and waste control reports can prove invaluable, for example, when a buyer is being challenged for paying a premium price for a particular product. As in other areas, the more information the buyer has at hand, the better the job he will be able to do.

WASTE REPORT

Product: _____

Pounds Received: _____

Pounds of trim removed
prior to use: _____

Usable Weight: _____

Note: This approach would be most applicable to the receipt of meat, poultry, or seafood which frequently must be trimmed prior to use. A different approach would be to measure and record drained weight (and hence weight loss) on items packed in water or ice upon receipt.

Figure 20

PAST PURCHASING ACTIVITY

Recording past purchasing activity builds a fund of information which can be used by the buyer in conducting future purchasing activities. Perhaps the simplest way of building this record is to keep a file of purchase orders broken down either by supplier or by product purchase. This will provide a ready reference point for the buyer who is looking for answers to such questions as, "What did I pay a year ago?" "What quantity makes the most logical purchase unit?" "How many suppliers are there for product X?" "What type of lead time is required for shipments?" While the owner and manager of the small food service operation may also be doing the buying and may therefore disregard this type of record keeping activity, generally such records help to increase the effectiveness of all buying activity.

An additional record you should include in your purchasing records is a supplier evaluation card. The card should record the comments both pro and con regarding each supplier's performance in providing a product to the organization. Comments from other parts of the organization such as receiving reports, quality control analyses, and yield and waste control reports should all be included in this supplier evaluation file. Such a file is particularly useful when there is a turnover in buying personnel and a new individual must come on the scene and attempt to assimilate information about past dealings with a particular vendor. Although this situation may not occur often, when it does, a file like this will prove invaluable.

PROJECTING FUTURE NEEDS

Another area of purchasing procedures and controls that is commonly overlooked is the importance of projecting future needs. While technically outside the province of the purchasing office, the projection of future needs is something that must be done by the operating areas of the company based on anticipated sales volumes. The results of these projections should be forwarded to the purchasing department for use in planning future purchase activity. If the buyer finds that this type of future planning is not taking place, he should contact operations personnel and insist that it be started. By cooperating with the operating people in developing these forecasts, the buyer will not only be increasing his service to the operational area of the company, but he will also be setting the stage for increasing his own effectiveness in making a purchase.

Another advantage of forecasting future needs is to give the buyer additional lead time to investigate a given item and to take advantage of cyclical price patterns. Strawberries, since they are harvested during late May and early June on the west coast, are normally most attractively priced at that time. Red meat, on the other hand, normally reaches its lowest price level during the fourth quarter of each calendar year. In both these cases projecting the requirements for the next twelve months will substantially enhance the buyer's ability to purchase these products on the most favorable price basis. While the buyer himself may not be in a position to determine what the operation's future needs will be, he can certainly encourage the operational people in his organization to estimate such future requirements.

PRICE FORECASTS

A final area of purchasing that is the full responsibility of the buyer is forecasting prices he expects to pay over fixed periods of time in the future. Once the buyer has received the requirements forecasts from the operating people, he must estimate the prices he expects to pay for these products in the future. Generally, these estimates should be broken down on a monthly or quarterly basis and should forecast anywhere from three to twelve months in the future. Obviously, the more distant the period of time of the projection, the greater the uncertainty in making it. However, and this is especially true in a large organization, accurate forecasts of future price activity can have a significant impact on the profitability of the organization. If the buyer has developed the ability to forecast prices with a fair degree of accuracy, his forecasts can be used by the operational people for such things as planning which items to feature on the menu. If the buyer forecasts that turkey prices will be up sharply during the next six months, the operations people can either increase the selling price of turkey, deemphasize it on the menu, or remove it entirely from the menu. On the other hand, if the buyer sees shrimp prices decreasing substantially over the next six months, he might recommend more emphasis on this particular item than is normally the custom in that operation.

Price forecasting is at best an inexact science. However, every buyer in the food service industry should take it upon himself to develop his skills in this area. A good way to begin is to make practice forecasts on the major commodity items which your organization uses. The buyer should begin immediately to list the important items which his firm purchases and then attempt to forecast the price he expects

Product		Jan	Feb	Mar	Apr	May	June
Chicken	Forecast						
	Actual						
Potatoes	Forecast						
	Actual						
Soybean Oil	Forecast						
	Actual						
Hamburger	Forecast						
	Actual						
Sugar	Forecast						
	Actual						

Figure 21

to pay for each of these items by month for a period of up to six months in the future. These forecasts should be made in writing and should be compared to the actual market price each month.

Figure 21 shows a typical form that can be used for this purpose. Note that below each forecasted price is a box where the actual price for the month can be inserted. By comparing the actual price to the forecasted price, the buyer can then do a self-evaluation of his forecasting ability. As he develops a higher degree of accuracy, he should begin turning these forecasts over to the operations people for their use in menu planning, profit planning, etc. He should also explain to the operations people that these forecasts represent his best judgment of what the market price will be at some point in the future, but that they should not be construed as a guarantee that the product will definitely be available at that price. The degree to which the buyer can help forecast price for the operations people will in large part determine how effectively other areas of the operation such as menu planning, long term purchasing, and inventory stockpiling will function.

The comments in this chapter are intended to highlight the major procedural and control techniques that should be used to whatever degree is useful in your food service purchasing operation. The degree to which each of these devices is used, however, rests with the individual responsible for the buying and with his immediate superiors. My suggestions are not designed to restrict the flexibility or fluidity of any purchasing operation. Rather, they show what these various techniques can offer in the way of improved purchasing performance.

Each food service buyer in each company will have to judge for himself the proper mix of these various procedures and control techniques. Probably the only organizational structure which would utilize every one of the items mentioned in this chapter in full detail would be the purchasing function of the very large national chain. However I felt that it was better that I detail each of these techniques and allow the reader to make his own selection (as one might from a good restaurant menu) as to the combination that appears best for his particular operation.

Once again I want to emphasize the point that a modification of each of these techniques will work for the individual restaurant operator or the very small multiunit operation.

Chapter 12 Questions

1. What are the minimum controls that you feel are necessary in a purchasing operation?

2. In your judgment, which of the purchasing controls is most important? Defend your choice.

3. Under what circumstances would you say that a requisition is an absolute necessity?

4. Assume a food service operation is using a receiving report. What areas of the operation should see copies of the receiving report? How should each of these areas make use of the receiving report?

5. Describe how a typical yield analysis and a typical waste control analysis might be conducted in a food service operation.

6. Prepare a simple outline of a format which you feel a buyer might use in preparing price projection. Include in the format an indication of the frequency of the projection, the total period of time to be covered, and the individuals to whom copies of the projection should be forwarded.

13

Training Purchasing Personnel

QUALITIES IMPORTANT IN PURCHASING

A frequently asked question in the food service industry is, "What makes a good buyer or purchasing agent?" There is no simple answer to this question. However, in this chapter I will try to provide some answers based upon my eighteen years of experience knowing and communicating with hundreds of purchasing people in the food service industry. Many of these answers will be generalizations based on the ideal qualities and ambitions of people who have been successful in purchasing segments of the food service industry.

I will also attempt to cover the types of training programs that are best for developing competent purchasing people and for maintaining updated job skills for those persons already engaged in the profession. This latter area is of increasing importance as costs continue to escalate along with the need for more innovative and creative approaches to the purchasing profession.

IMPORTANT CHARACTERISTICS

A purchasing person should be one who recognizes the tremendous opportunity for profit improvement which can be generated by a well-executed purchasing program. He is naturally inquisitive, skilled in analytic evaluations, forceful but reasonable in his dealings with other people, and committed to a higher level of performance. Obviously, the characteristics of honesty, integrity, intelligence, self-discipline, and thoroughness also apply to any candidate looking for a purchasing job in a food service operation. The candidate's willingness to spend a great deal of time developing sources of supply and making certain that his employer receives the maximum value for each dollar expended is also of critical importance.

Purchasing is a very demanding profession. It is not for those who are poorly motivated and need a great deal of prodding. In fact, people selected for the purchasing department should be proven performers in some other area of business or schooling. It is best if they know at the outset that the job is demanding and that they will be expected to maintain a high level of performance in order to keep their job. To aid them in their performance, you should carefully instruct them in the purchasing philosophy and policy of the particular organization, be it a family owned restaurant or a major multi-unit national chain.

Once the individual has been selected as a possible candidate for a purchasing position, the management should make every effort to acquaint him with all facets of the business. It is not sufficient for a purchasing person to handle the daily procurement chores in a vacuum, insulated from all the other activities of the operation. He should be aware of the menu planning philosophy of the firm, the frequency with which the menu is modified, and the gross profit (balance remaining after the cost of the food is subtracted from the menu selling price) objectives which management is striving to achieve.

The gross profit figure is of special importance to the buyer or purchasing agent, since it is so directly influenced by changes in the price of food either up or down. If the buyer is acquainted with the menu philosophy and gross profit target, he can more effectively recommend the addition or deletion of items from the menu, depending on their price changes. Similarly, if the buyer is employed by a larger chain which may have some of its own manufacturing operations, he must be fully exposed to all facets of those manufacturing activities. He should participate in whatever weekly or monthly meetings are held within the manufacturing area to discuss production schedules, inventory levels, product modification, etc. In fact, his advice should be considered in every manufacturing decision made.

Obviously a newcomer to the field of purchasing should not be forced into a decision-making position until he has developed sufficient grasp of the various problems he will encounter on the job. Rather than consider the pros and cons of various training systems—a subject of great dispute—I would like to tell you about the purchasing training program that worked for me when I began my career in food buying eighteen years ago, and which I in turn have used successfully with a score of purchasing people in the intervening years.

ONE SUCCESSFUL TRAINING PROGRAM

The Initial Briefing

Let's assume that we have an individual who shows the necessary personal and intellectual requisites for the job. The first step is to outline to this person in as much detail as possible the basic purchasing philosophy of the company and the individual to whom he will report. During this initial briefing, the interviewer should be sensitive to any questions or confusions the trainee might have. Frequently, questions come up during this time. Rather than dismissing such queries or answering them in brief, the interviewer should answer them in considerable detail at the time they are raised. By encouraging questions, the trainer can get an insight into the trainee's level of understanding. This insight can help determine the pace and level of the training program to follow.

PROCEDURAL ASPECTS OF PURCHASING

Once the basic phliosophy has been covered, the procedural aspects of the purchasing job must be considered. This can take anywhere from several weeks to several months for completion and should focus on the fundamental operating procedures of the purchasing function.

No detail, no matter how routine, should be omitted from this initial procedural briefing. All paperwork techniques should be covered in enough detail to give the trainee a thorough understanding of this area. These include the use of requisitions, purchase orders, shipping instructions, receiving reports, quality control inspection forms, invoice approval documents, accounts payable transmittal forms, payment vouchers, and company checks forwarded to the vendor in payment for goods or services rendered. Of equal importance is an examination of such purchasing procedures as minimum and maximum order quantities, minimum and maximum inventory levels, product specifications, order frequencies, quality control test procedures, etc. While a listing of these various items may seem somewhat unnecessary to the casual observer, it is my experience that these most fundamental aspects of the purchasing practice are frequently overlooked because both trainer and trainee are impatient to get on with the actual assimilation of purchasing knowledge by the new employee.

Three Further Training Stages

After these fundamentals have been mastered, there are really three stages of the training function still to come: First, a period of "sitting at the elbow" of an experienced buyer in order to learn by seeing; second, a period of visiting the manufacturing facilities of major suppliers in order to see firsthand how products are manufactured, packaged, stored, and shipped; and third, a period of actually buying on one's own with the knowledge that an experienced hand is available at any time should a question or problem arise. Let us consider each of these three stages in more detail.

During the looking and listening stage the trainee should be primarily a silent observer. His purpose is to observe his trainer as well as the vendors in working out a purchase agreement. At the close of each transaction or at the close of each business day, the trainer should set aside sufficient time to discuss each of the day's transactions with the trainee. During these discussion periods the trainee should be given ample opportunity to ask any questions he has about the transaction. Even more important, he should be asked to give his impressions of what he observed. It is not enough to simply ask the trainee if he has any questions. It is also important that the trainer request feedback from the trainee so that he is able to see how much the trainee is absorbing.

By this time you are undoubtedly wondering, "How long should this 'learning by seeing' process continue?" There is no "right" answer to this question. It depends on the individual trainer and trainee, and on the particular job for which the trainee is being prepared. However, after some period of time which is usually shorter, rather than longer, than expected, both the trainer and the trainee will look at one another and by mutual consent decide that the time has come to move on to the next stage.

The next phase in the training of the food service buyer is the supplier and product exposure phase. During this period the trainee concentrates his full efforts on direct exposure to the products, processes, and personnel of key supplier organizations. This may involve a short visit to the local wholesale produce market at three o'clock in the morning, a week in the cutting room of a local food service industry meat purveyor wearing a white coat and hard hat, multiple tours through various freezers in the area, sitting with the office manager of a large china, glass, and flatware distributor, or riding with the driver of a local paper supply warehouse as he makes his rounds to various food service customers.

When I first joined Howard Johnson's after ten years in another segment of the food industry, the first thing I did to "learn the business" was to spend a week working in a restaurant kitchen. A better crash course in what the food service industry is all about has not yet been developed. If a purchasing trainee has any real flair for the job, he will feast on the opportunity to get this firsthand exposure to existing suppliers and their products and processes. It is an excellent way to assimilate a tremendous amount of information in a very short period of time.

You will find that most supplier organizations are delighted to cooperate in the implementation of a training program of this type. They welcome the opportunity to present their company and their story to a fresh, hopefully unbiased, and totally objective mind. I have found that when supplier organizations have been asked to participate in this type of training, they are not only responsive, but also careful not to abuse the trust which has been placed in them. Once again, the question of how long this phase of the training cycle must be answered on an individual basis. As a general guideline, however, I would suggest that this phase of the training cycle can be accomplished in a two- to four-week period.

The final phase in the development of the new food service buyer is what I call "on-the-job baptism by fire." During this period the new buyer actually begins his constructive effort on behalf of his employer. His trainer begins to assign specific purchasing responsibilities to him for execution. At first these responsibilities may be relatively minor assignments such as calling a new supplier to inquire if he carries product X, asking an existing supplier for a current price quotation, calling a purveyor to rearrange a planned delivery, checking with a regulatory agency to obtain information on a particular regulatory requirement, or even interviewing a sales person who had the poor taste to call on the company without an appointment. It is remarkable how quickly these very mundane assignments set the foundation for a gradual and yet very natural transition into more productive buying activities. By approaching the more important activities step-by-step, the shock of total immersion into the purchasing function is significantly reduced.

Knowing that volumes have been written on the art of training, I will not attempt to suggest that the thoughts contained in this chapter represent the ultimate answer to the age-old question of how does one train one's fellow man. Rather, these thoughts are a synthesis of one person's experience in training purchasing people for the food and food service industries, and as such, may provide some useful guidelines for application in your own specific training situation.

Chapter 13 Questions

1. What qualifications would you suggest as a minimum requirement for a person who wishes to enter the purchasing profession in the food service industry?

2. What are the three stages in buying training after the basic procedural orientation has been accomplished?

3. Why are supplier contacts and plant visitations such an important part of the purchasing training program?

4. How would you determine whether a prospective buyer has developed sufficient understanding of his job responsibilities to permit the actual buying responsibility to be turned over to him?

5. How can a buyer expand and supplement his purchasing training on a continuing basis?

14

Purchasing and Quality Control

HOW THEY RELATE

The relationship between the purchasing function and the quality control department in a small restaurant may be as fundamental as the owner deciding before he makes a purchase that he is only going to buy Grade A vegetables, choice meat, or 26–30 count shrimp, and then going ahead and making the purchase. Since the buyer and the quality control person are one and the same, there can be no disagreement between the two as to acceptable quality levels. The situation in the multiunit chain operation or in the giant national food service corporations, however, may be drastically different. As soon as a restaurant organization gets to a sufficient size to justify assigning responsibility for quality control to someone outside the purchasing function, the initial storm clouds may begin to gather.

Remember that quality control, while an ongoing responsibility of the purchasing function, is not, and should never be, the ultimate responsibility of the buyer. As in government, an organization with a system of checks and balances functions more efficiently than one without such checks. If the quality control function were the ultimate responsibility of the purchasing department, a very critical checkpoint would be eliminated, since there would be no one other than the buyer to check on the quality of the merchandise he himself purchased. This is simply not a sound business practice.

Depending upon the size of the operation, quality control may include any number of requirements. In a small operation where the owner shoulders the responsibility, it involves one person who spends a small percentage of his time checking incoming food receipts. In the larger chains, it may consist of a multiemployee department dispersed over a wide geographical area with individual specialists responsible for specific commodities or commodity groups, and others who devote their efforts to supplier plant visitations, ongoing relationships with government regulatory authorities, etc. Regardless of the size of the quality control function, the buyer or the purchasing department must have a constant and trusting relationship with the quality control function. Good relationships between these two areas can result in significantly more efficient procurement activities. Poor relationships result in either inferior quality merchandise or in superior quality merchandise when average quality is sufficient. Even worse, relationships with suppliers are damaged if the vendors become unwitting pawns in a war between the purchasing and quality control functions.

In one well-known company, the man responsible for doing the buying felt that he knew more about quality control than anyone else, and that if he considered a particular item satisfactory, no one else in the company could challenge his decision. This attitude had worked satisfactorily during the early days of the company, when their fifteen operations were all located within a 100 mile radius of a major city, and when the company obtained most food requirements from vendors who could serve all units.

However, as the company grew and opened units throughout the United States, supply patterns changed. As new points of supply were developed, complaints from operators and customers grew louder about the variation in the quality of the food served in the chain's various local units. Moreover, the fact that this company made little use of frozen food aggravated the problem still further. Finally, the management assigned responsibility for quality control to one of their senior operating people and asked him to monitor on a random sample basis receipts of various food products at the chain's different units around the country.

The initial results of this sampling showed that not only did the company need substantially tighter product specifications, but they also needed a program of supplier education in order to assure compliance with the specifications. When the quality control man approached the purchasing man with this recommendation, the purchasing man took it as a personal affront and criticism of his job performance and promptly rejected the suggestions. Determined to "show up that quality control character," he deliberately bought a truckload of frozen beef to use for hamburgers when the product specifications required that only fresh beef could be used. In the purchasing man's narrow prospective, he felt that by insisting on the out of spec load of product, he could finally prove the superiority of the purchasing function. Much to his chagrin, management backed the quality control man on his recommendation to forego using frozen beef in the company's hamburger product until extensive testing and specification modification had been completed. (The purchasing man was reprimanded and subsequently forced into early retirement.)

During this struggle the supplier of the frozen beef was put through the unnecessary aggravation of delivering his product, having it rejected by the quality control department, and then having to fight with the purchasing agent to recover his added expense for the rejected shipment, which would have been absolutely satisfactory to any customer who regularly used frozen meat.

Obviously, the confrontation just described is not the way to build a harmonious relationship between the purchasing and quality control functions in a food service operation. Because it is one of the key operating relationships in the entire organization, the relations between these two departments should be watched by senior management to insure harmony and cooperation.

GOOD WORKING RELATIONSHIPS

Now that we have seen how poor relationships can harm the company both internally and externally, the next question is how to develop an optimum working relationship between purchasing and quality control. Simply stated, the foundation for this relationship rests on total disclosure from both sides. The purchasing department should always involve quality control at the earliest possible time in any decision or preliminary negotiation which involves a new product or supplier to the company. This would include such occurrences as a supplier's recommendation for a new or modified product, a new supplier's response to an inquiry about his product line, or a recommendation from the operations people to investigate a competitor's product.

Since the relationship between purchasing and quality control is a critical one, to function most effectively, there must be mutual, continuous, and ongoing communication. Just as purchasing must inform quality control of its goings-on, quality control (also called "quality assurance") must also maintain an open line of communication with the purchasing department.

This is especially important when quality control considers a product unacceptable under existing company specifications. Purchasing should receive immediate notification of this fact. The best time to deal with any quality problem is immediately upon receipt of the merchandise. A delay of even 24 hours with a perishable product can sharply reduce the degree of satisfaction which can be obtained from the vendor, since he will claim that the deterioration occurred during the 24-hour delay period. The quality control person or department must understand that the purchasing person has no way of knowing how the merchandise is received unless this information is conveyed by quality control. While he has a definite responsibility for the arrival of merchandise in acceptable condition, he is not responsible for actually inspecting it at the time of arrival, and therefore must be notified if there is a problem.

The quality control department should also be given the opportunity to participate in discussions with various vendors when quality problems come up. This discussion may be as simple as a telephone conversation with the vendor in order to review product specifications, or as involved as a plant visit to the vendor's operation in order to inspect the manufacturing process to determine where problems, if any, are originating.

VENDOR REACTION

No chapter on the relationships between purchasing and quality control would be complete without a comment on how the vendor views this relationship. While the great majority of vendors welcomes a thorough and objective appraisal of their products by their customer's quality control function, a considerable number will react with surprising hostility if they believe that they are not getting a fair appraisal. There is nothing more distasteful to a vendor than to have his product unjustly evaluated by a customer's quality control operation. If you are aware of such a practice taking place in your organization, regardless of the reason, you should do whatever you can to eliminate it as soon as possible. Allowing it to continue severely damages vendor relationships.

On the other hand, there are certain vendors who will determine precisely what degree of quality control inspection the customer employs. Having "built a book" on that particular customer's quality control procedures, these vendors will then ship accordingly. The customer with the accurate scale gets the accurate weight; the customer with the inaccurate scale, or only intermittent weight checks, gets the vendor's option on weights. The customer who makes a random count check on every case of produce gets the proper count; the one who does not bother receives pot luck—usually not in his favor.

COUNT

In discussing quality control, people frequently overlook count as one of the important measuring tools of quality. If a case of liquor contains only eleven bottles, this is a quality as well as a quantity deficiency. While people think of count as a measure of quantity rather than quality, there are so many items sold to the food service industry on a count basis (26–30 count shrimp, a dozen eggs, a case of twelve bottles of catsup, a crate of lettuce with a fixed number of heads, a case of twelve bottles of scotch) that quality control must include quantity as well.

Because there are so many different ways in which quality control deficiencies can develop, the food service buyer should develop an early instinct for building quality control considerations into purchasing decisions. A good buyer gets to the point where, in his initial discussions with a new supplier, he can tell almost immediately if he is going to have quality control problems. In the case of the larger chain he will also be able to develop a feel for the consistency of his own operations people: Are their quality control objectives always the same? Or do they vary depending upon how badly the product is needed or how competitive the price is at any given point in time?

EACH TO HIS OWN

A famous man once observed that any item is worth whatever someone will pay for it. In other words, value is a relative thing. It depends on how a person views the worth of an object. In many ways quality is also relative. Prime beef is widely acknowledged to provide the ultimate in a beef eating experience. But it would be most inappropriate if your local fast food restaurant served it to you, since the fast food restaurant usually chooses to sell a hamburger manufactured from beef that would grade U.S. Good at best. This does not in any way suggest that that establishment is serving substandard quality beef. It simply means that a different quality of beef is appropriate for a hamburger stand than for a fine steak house. Both establishments must have a dedication to quality control if they are to succeed in the competitive marketplace. However, quality control guidelines for each must be developed relative to their individual product mix, the type of customer they serve, and the price of the menu.

Thus each food service establishment must develop its own quality control program that is specifically geared to its needs. Other than the rule that no establishment should ever be allowed to serve spoiled food, it is impossible to generalize about a quality control program that will be suitable for all food service establishments. If you establishment has not already determined exactly what its quality control program will be and communicated this information to its purchasing function, it should be done without further delay. It will then be the responsibility of the purchasing department to communicate the quality control requirements to each vendor, and to serve as a conduit between quality control and the vendor to insure that what is required is in fact delivered.

Chapter 14 Questions

1. Describe the optimum relationship that should exist between the purchasing and quality control functions.

2. Why is it important for negative quality reports to be communicated to the purchasing department immediately?

3. At what point in the purchasing negotiation with a vendor should the quality control requirements be communicated to the vendor?

4. Describe some of the ways in which a vendor can take advantage of a food service firm that does not monitor quality control.

5. Why must quality control programs be geared individually for each food service operation?

15

Service and Vendor Relations

CHECKING ON A VENDOR'S RELIABILITY

In many purchasing situations the buyer's responsibility does not end when the goods are delivered to him. If he is looking for some special service or training program, he must insure that these services are also provided. No one wants to be responsible for having dealt with a disreputable food service equipment dealer who sells a particular product with a 24 hour per day, seven day per week service guarantee and then refuses to service when a need comes up.

If a buyer is purchasing items that have an ongoing service or training responsibility from the vendor, the best way to check on how well a vendor fulfills his responsibility is to talk with other customers. Frequently these customers will point out problem areas that the buyer should know about before deciding whether or not to enter into a purchase relationship with this vendor.

At the time a supplier makes a sales presentation for any item that requires future service (usually some type of equipment such as a toaster, a coffee urn, a new walk-in refrigerator, or a slicing machine), he should be asked for a written statement of his service capabilities and service commitments. When competitive quotations from various suppliers come in, their service programs should be evaluated and compared on a competitive basis, just as the quality and price of their items are.

As many buyers of food service equipment will sadly attest, the dishwashing machine which looked like the best buy because of its price turned out to be a costly error when it developed mechanical problems. Generally, if a buyer finds that a particular food material is defective in quality, he has sufficient backup stock to be able to set the defective product aside and continue the operation without interruption. However, very few food service establishments carry backup equipment for such things as dishwashing machines, walk-in refrigerators, or coffee urns, so if one of these units turns out to be defective on any kind of a regular pattern, the entire operation may well be interrupted.

Although experience is usually the best teacher in this phase of food service buying, you can always improve your chances of success by checking the supplier's reliability and capability with other customers, and by getting written commitments from the supplier as to the specifics of his service program. Most reputable suppliers welcome the opportunity to insure that all customers are satisfied with the product they have purchased. If a buyer has a complaint or question about a product that he has purchased, he should contact the supplier and request a follow-up sales/service call.

REQUEST FOLLOW-UP CALLS

In this day of increasing use of frozen prepared food, reconstitution procedures can be a very important ingredient in the success of a product. If the buyer finds that his operations people or customers are dissatisfied with a particular product, it is entirely possible that the kitchen help are not following all the reconstitution instructions. This would be an excellent example of a time when the vendor sales person should be asked to return and provide very specific assistance in resolving a product problem. It may simply be that the reconstitution instructions are somewhat unclear. But it is also possible that there is a specific problem with the product which the vendor should be aware of.

BUY EASY-TO-OPERATE EQUIPMENT

When evaluating vendor equipment service programs, the buyer should also consider the complexity of the operating instructions for a given piece of equipment. Many people say that products and equipment should be "idiot proof" so they insure ease of operation at the point of use. This description is not in any way intended to denigrate the people operating the equipment. Rather, it expresses the desire to eliminate any unnecessary complexities. A piece of kitchen equipment which requires a very complex set of cleaning instructions in order to avoid repeated breakdowns and consequent service calls is probably not the right piece of equipment for the average food service operation. It is unrealistic to expect kitchen personnel who frequently are overworked and underpaid, and who may even have a language barrier to have the time or ability to follow complex instructions to the letter.

The buyer should be aware that service calls, even from a company which has maintained a good service program, mean that you are losing unnecessary time and money because of any temporary halts. The objective of a service program is to have it available when needed. But even more important is not to need that service at all. If the buyer feels that a piece of equipment is too complex for his operating people, he should not purchase it, no matter how comprehensive the service program included.

VENDOR RELATIONS

Another very important factor in the purchasing profession is the broad area of vendor relations. Vendor relations means different abilities and services to different buyers. To some buyers, it means they have the ability to extract a maximum amount of incremental service from their vendors without having to pay for it. To others, it means developing the kind of relationship with a supplier that when the supplier tells him about the quality or performance of his product, the buyer can accept that statement's truth and does not have to double check it for himself. In between these two extremes is a wide spectrum of buyer/vendor relationships, any one of which can have an important impact on the purchasing job which the buyer is doing for his employer.

When properly motivated and rewarded, a firm's vendors can be its most important ally in a time of procurement difficulty. These difficulties run the gamut from product shortages and rapid changes in price to government intervention in the supply pattern on a given product during a commodity embargo. The buyer who has been working with his vendors and has treated them fairly and earned their respect consistently outshines his fellow buyers when such problems arise. This is directly related to, and dependent upon, his relationship with his suppliers. A supplier who has been fairly treated by a buyer will be likely to extend himself to whatever degree he possibly can to help that buyer in a time of difficulty.

DON'T MISINTERPRET SUPPLIER COME-ONS

Too many buyers in the food service industry tend to develop an inflated idea of their own importance because of the attention that suppliers give them when trying to get the order. Any purchasing person who is naive enough to be misled by this attention does not deserve the responsibility which the buying job involves. Next to a lack of integrity, the most serious error a buyer can make is interpreting this attention as anything other than a legitimate attempt to get the order. If the buyer thinks that his sparkling personality, fine intellect, or good looks are attracting the supplier's attention, he is sadly mistaken. Human nature being what it is, it is easy to understand how a buyer can be misled. However, he should brace himself against these temptations and recognize that without the objectivity to see these come-ons for what they are, his efficiency and objectivity will be severely reduced.

Notwithstanding the pitfalls of vendor relations, success in dealing with vendors can significantly enhance the quality of a buyer's job. There is absolutely nothing wrong with forming a more personal relationship and talking about subjects other than business. However, at all times the buyer must remember the fundamental reason why they are together. He must not allow any other considerations to get in the way of that transaction. He should keep in mind that a sales person who can bring in other considerations may be doing so at the buyer's expense.

Just because a sales person attempts to do this, however, does not necessarily mean that he is an incompetent representative. Different people have different methods of getting the same job done. During my purchasing career I have known and worked with a wide variety of sales people. They ranged from a man who presented such a hard sell that I became physically tired after ten minutes of listening to him, to a low-key salesman who hardly even mentioned his product except in the most apologetic fashion. I have known sales people who were extremely effective and those who were not. Every sales person has his own individual technique for selling his products. While we might wish that all sales people would give an objective presentation of their product, very few actually do.

"DO UNTO OTHERS . . ."

The good buyer should be able to use his sales contacts in the most effective way possible. He should develop a relationship with them which is founded on mutual trust and respect. When he gives his word to a sales representative, it should be his bond, and if he is not absolutely certain of his ability to keep his word, it should not be given in the first place. Similarly, the sales person should treat his buyer with equal consideration. Once he makes a commitment, the buyer has every right to expect that it will be kept. If it is not, unless there are extenuating circumstances, the buyer should discontinue his relationship with this vendor as soon as possible.

BUYER RESPONSIBILITIES TO THE VENDOR

In discussing the subjects of commitment and performance on both sides of the purchase and sales transaction, we must also remember that there is another area which is a critical element in developing good buying technique. This is the area of buyer responsibility. This requires that the buyer understand precisely what he is expected to buy and that he communicate precisely this information to the vendor's sales representative. Thus, if the buyer is asked to purchase nothing but extra-long fancy Grade A French fries cut $5/8$ of an inch thick and the buyer communicates to the vendor that he is interested in buying simply Grade A long French fries, we have an immediate problem.

Communication is a very difficult and demanding science, particularly when words are used to describe very different product characteristics. It is absolutely essential that the buyer communicate precisely and completely the specifications of the product he wishes to purchase. To help do this, consider the old Army directive, "Verbal orders don't go; put it in writing." The very best way for a buyer to communicate product specifications to a potential vendor is in writing.

Chapter 15 Questions

1. What elements should a buyer include in negotiating a service program with a vendor?

2. How can the buyer best communicate the elements of the service program to his field operations people?

3. What benefits can a buyer expect to receive as a result of a good vendor relations program?

4. What steps should a buyer take to develop a vendor relations program?

5. How should a buyer react to a vendor who does not honor commitments previously made?

16

Value Analysis As a Purchasing Tool

VALUE ANALYSIS: A DEFINITION

During the 1960's the most popular phrase in the general industrial purchasing field was *value analysis*. I suspect that more purchasing seminars and speeches concentrated on that subject than any other single topic for a decade. Value analysis is nothing more than a refinement of the long-standing purchasing approach that the buyer should attempt to get the best buy for his money. In value analysis, the person doing the studying (naturally referred to as the *value analyst*) dissects each segment of the particular purchase transaction to determine if in fact the best possible value is being received for the money.

While the basic concepts of value analysis have always made sense, their application to the food service industry did not really begin until the early 1970's. Since the food service industry tended to be primarily operations oriented, the cost of purchases was treated loosely as long as sales were good and profits were strong. However, the escalating food costs and frozen menu prices of 1973 developed a new outlook in a remarkably short period of time. All of a sudden operations-oriented people who had largely ignored such mundane matters as meat prices and produce costs began to take detailed looks at these areas.

At this point, value analysis in the restaurant industry really came into being. Necessity demanded that each food service establishment get the maximum return for each dollar expended. Since there was little that the industry could do to stem the ever-upward movement of labor, utility, and occupancy costs, food cost became the primary target area, and the concepts of value analysis became the most popular pastime of our industry. How does it work in the food service industry? Let's take a look at a few examples which will help you apply this concept to your specific establishment.

PRICE VALUE RELATIONSHIP

We have all become accustomed to the idea that the better the quality, the higher the price. However, there is frequently more to the equation than just price and value (quality). Now we also look at *yield,* or the amount of usable product generated by each pound of food purchased. Ten pounds of raw potatoes will yield approximately four pounds of preblanched French fries ready for the deep fryer. Ten pounds of flounder will yield fourteen pounds of breaded fish fillets when combined with a 40% breading mix. A thirty-pound primal rib, when properly trimmed for oven roasting, will yield about twenty-one pounds of product before cooking and some sixteen pounds after cooking.

What is the impact of these various yields on the price paid for the initial raw material? Should the buyer and the user consider alternate materials that may be higher or lower priced, but will have greater or lesser yields? What is the best combination of factors such as price, quality, yield, labor, handling time, waste, customer satisfaction, and storage qualities that can be developed for a given raw material? This is where the value analyst comes into his own. He is the one who will take each of these factors, define it as carefully as possible, and then put together a composite picture showing the optimum combination of factors for his firm.

Since most food service organizations, even the large national chains, are not broadly enough staffed to have a separate value analysis department, responsibility for this task may lie with the purchasing department, the operations area, or, in the case of a company manufacturing its own food products in a commissary system, a manufacturing or financial analyst.

Based on my own experience, I have seen this responsibility best executed when it involves all of these areas, and when the analysis is carried out on a project-by-project basis. I have found that, even though only one person assumes basic responsibility for the value analysis, if the input is generated from a number of different areas, the final decisions or findings tend to be more accurate and meaningful. Some people may ask, "Why bother involving other areas of the corporation when value analysis activities are essentially geared to insure maximum return for each purchasing dollar expended?" While on the surface this may seem to be the entire story, in actuality many of the key elements in the value analyst's decision-making process are totally outside the control of the purchasing function.

For example, by investigating product specifications versus product requirements, the value analyst may find that a particular product spec is far more demanding and hence, more expensive, than necessary. A fried chicken operation that had a specification calling for boneless chicken breasts would certainly be incurring unnecessarily excessive costs. While most situations in the food service industry are not that obvious, there are many times when an unnecessary specification has been imposed, through lack of information about alternative raw material availabilities, new product developments, or new and more modern processing capabilities.

The person charged with the value analysis responsibility cannot be expected to stay abreast of all this information by himself. This is why it is so important for other area to contribute input and information. The best way to insure such input and analysis on an ongoing basis is to establish a value analysis team who will cover the specific projects on a regular basis. This team should have a leader who clearly understands his responsibility to execute all phases of the value analysis task and to motivate the other team members in providing whatever input is necessary to accomplish this goal.

Be very careful not to confuse value analysis strictly with the measurement of purchasing efficiency. Certainly efficiency is one of its major areas of activity. But there are other areas of equal, or perhaps even more important, impact on the company. Yield analysis, specification evaluation, and alternate product development significantly affect the firm's price value relationships.

MEASURING PURCHASING EFFICIENCY

Before developing these other areas further, let us consider that segment of value analysis which is the measurement of purchasing efficiency. Every food service operation, from the smallest independently owned restaurant to the major chain, should have an ongoing analysis of its purchasing efficiency as a regular procedure in its operation. This analysis might involve something as simple as a discussion with a fellow restaurant operator in another part of town comparing prices being paid for certain major ingredients, or as sophisticated as computer evaluations of major commodity purchases to track the actual prices paid by the purchasing department against market price movement. Because the purchasing department is in the unique position of spending the company's money, it is particularly important that its actions be the subject of constant scrutiny.

One activity that bears particular attention is buying certain products only from certain suppliers. In the vast majority of cases this is the result of the buyer's feeling confident that if he does business with a limited number of suppliers whom he knows through past business association, he can count on them for good quality, good service, and a generally competitive price. To his uninitiated coworker this may appear to be sloppy purchasing. The impression this creates in the mind of other employees as well can be as troublesome as if it were actually true.

Thus, one of the most important responsibilities of the value analyst is to constantly challenge existing purchasing relationships in order to reconfirm the value of continuing them. Naturally, the responsibility for this type of value analysis cannot and should not be assigned to the same individual who has the buying responsibility. In the smaller operation where purchasing is handled by someone other than the owner/manager, then this responsibility should rest with the owner/manager. An important side benefit of the owner/manager's involving himself in this type of value analysis is the learning experience which he will gain from it. Conducting the value analysis examination will expose him to purchasing information which he might not otherwise know about.

TIMING EFFICIENCY

One important measure of the efficiency of the purchasing department is the timing efficiency of purchasing activity; i.e., comparing the purchase price of specific items with their price activity. As a random evaluation of timing efficiency, the value analyst might select two or three major items purchased during a thirty day period. He would then chart the prices paid for these items each time they were purchased during the period. On the same chart, he should then enter the high and low price quotation for these items each week. He is then in a position to compare the price actually paid with the high and low price quoted for that item. If he sees that the actual purchase price tends to be at or above (heaven forbid) the market quotations during the period, he can conclude fairly safely that his buyer's sense of market timing could stand considerable improvement. If, however, this examination indicates that the actual price paid tends to be close to the low price quotation for the period, then he can assume that his buyer has a fairly good sense of market timing.

This type of analysis is particularly important in the larger company that enters into extended term price commitments where a given commodity may be purchased at a fixed price in sufficient quantity to last for three, six, twelve months or more. This type of purchase can have a very substantial impact on corporate profits if it turns out to be substantially under or over the average market price. Even in the single unit food service operation, however, the owner/manager will find it helpful to keep a chart of prices paid for the three or four largest dollar expenditure items in order to be able to compare the efficiency of the purchasing operation, and to have price records over an extended period of time for comparison purposes.

Just within the last couple of years there have been dramatic examples of how the price of common food items fluctuate. During 1974 when the price of sugar escalated from 15¢ a pound to 65¢ a pound, many food service operators and confectioners supplying the food service industry were caught in such a margin squeeze that they were forced to sharply curtail, or in some cases even discontinue, the use of the product. The price pressure became so severe that some restaurant customers actually began taking sugar packets home. This caused some restaurant chains to remove their sugar packets from the table and dole them out to customers only as requested.

Now that sugar prices have come back into more reasonable range, people speculate as to whether or not that type of price run-up can occur again. The answer is unequivocably, "Yes." In fact, it can occur with any commodity where the laws of supply and demand are in effect. The degree to which it occurs varies, of course. But regardless of the variations, commodity prices are subject primarily to the laws of supply and demand unless there is some artificial stimulus or deterrent such as government price supports.

Even such a mundane, everyday product as bacon went through a doubling of price during 1975 as the price of pork bellies (the raw material from which bacon is sliced) ran up from the low 50¢ per pound range to approximately $1.05 per pound. When this kind of rise happens, the food service operator has but two choices: 1) He can cut the portion, which is pretty difficult to do when you're only serving three strips of bacon to begin with, or, 2) he can increase the price. Let's face it though: Just because the price of bacon doubles doesn't mean that he can double the price of a bacon and egg breakfast. Admittedly, the bacon cost is only a portion of the total food cost in the bacon and egg breakfast. However, when there are 22 strips of bacon to a pound, and the per pound price goes from $1.05 to $2.10, those three strips suddenly cost the food service operator 30¢, which makes them the dominant cost factor in the entire breakfast.

I could ramble on for pages with additional specific examples of rapid and surprising food service raw material price advances and declines. However, these two suffice to point out that since considerable price variations do occur, usually without warning, the astute food service buyer must be prepared at all times to deal with them in the most profitable and effective way possible.

Chapter 16 Questions

1. How would you define *value analysis?*

2. What factors should be considered in performing a value analysis on a beef item to be used in a restaurant operation?

3. How can the alert buyer utilize the concepts of value analysis in his daily procurement activities?

4. Discuss how the concepts of value analysis can be used to measure the efficiency of the purchasing function.

5. In addition to lower prices, what are some of the other benefits to be derived from performing a value analysis on various items being purchased?

17

Communications

THE IMPORTANCE OF COMMUNICATING

It has been my experience that, even though a person may have the highest possible level of performance, it may be considered unsatisfactory unless his coworkers understand what he is doing and why. The magic ingredient here is communications. Although communications difficulties tend to increase geometrically as the size of an organization grows, the basic communications techniques have equal application in both the single and multiunit food service operation. The basic difference is the number of people who are involved in the communications. In the single unit operation the communicator has a relatively small number of people with whom he is communicating. In the larger organization, on the other hand, the number of people receiving the communication may be so large as to demand written rather than verbal communications.

GUIDELINES TO FOLLOW

The first and fundamental guideline for the buyer is: Make sure that everyone else knows what you are doing and why you are doing it. There are two basic reasons for this. First, it shows people that your intentions are open and honest. It is an unfortunate fact that many people outside the buying profession view buyers as people who use their job for personal benefit, and who ask, "What's in it for me?" before making every buying decision. While some buyers do conduct their jobs in this way, the vast majority are professionals who take great pride in doing their job honestly and well. Being clear about your intentions dismisses any suspicions about the way you carry on your business and gives others a better, more secure feeling about working with you.

A second important reason for being open about your intentions involves the flow of communications to and from the purchasing area. With the increasing importance of the purchasing function, purchasing people must rely more and more on other areas of the firm for information and assistance. This requires that other areas of the company be fully aware of the activities of the purchasing department. To insure a clear and continued flow of information, it is essential that these areas be informed about what the purchasing function is planning for the present and future.

Suppose, for example, that the buying function has prepared a budget forecast of prices which they expect to pay. Since this forecast was probably a major determinant of menu selling prices, any significant variations from the forecast will have a direct impact on profits, depending on how adequately and accurately menu prices jive with the prices actually paid. This is why purchasers must regularly compare prices actually paid against the budget forecast and against current menu prices. If the current menu results in profits below acceptable margins, then clearly menu prices need to be raised. Since the food cost is the largest and most dominant single factor on profit margins, all links in the purchasing chain must be alert to variations and required corrections. Unless purchasing is direct and clear about its intentions and requirements, the information which needs to be gathered and relayed will be hindered.

The buyer is usually the first person to receive the first early warning signal of price change. If he is not alert and does not immediately communicate the relevant information to all those who need to know, valuable time can be lost before the appropriate reactions to the price change are made. I cannot emphasize strongly enough the communications responsibility that rests on the person doing the buying. Since he is often the company's primary link with the outside marketplace, he alone is responsible for his company's awareness of, and reaction to, outside market conditions.

The classic and unfortunate example of poor communications from buyer to operations people occurred several years ago in a medium sized fast food chain where the marketing people and outside advertising agency came out with a new promotion (supported by television and radio advertising) offering two chicken dinners for the price of one. While the idea may have had great merit, the timing was abysmal. Just as the promotion broke, the price of chicken suddenly rose sharply. This rise, although surprising to the operations people, could have been predicted by the purchasing people. Unfortunately, because they were never contacted by marketing, purchasing could not offer input that would have avoided significant and unnecessary loss.

PURCHASING COMMUNICATIONS WITH OTHER AREAS

Communications with Financial People

In order for a food service operation to operate successfully, purchasing must regularly convey several kinds of information to the financial department. The most important of these comes in the form of a *purchase order,* which lists the quantity and price of all items being purchased. A purchase order is required before the financial area can process invoices from the vendors. (See pp. 149–150.)

When dispersing this information to the appropriate departments, at least one copy of each and every purchase order should be forwarded to a designated individual in the financial area. This can be put into a follow-up file so that if the merchandise requested is not received, it can be tracked down by Accounts Payable. Although it may be hard to believe that a vendor will accept a purchase order and then fail to ship the merchandise ordered, it actually happens with surprising frequency.

In addition to purchase order information, the buyer should also be transmitting forecasts of future prices which he expects to pay. These price forecasts, frequently referred to as the *purchasing budget,* are essential for preparing both sales budgets and profit and loss plans for the food service operation. Experience will dictate how detailed these price forecasts should become, but as a general rule, at least the top fifty items (in terms of total dollar value purchased per year) should be included in the purchasing area's price forecast.

To be most meaningful, this forecast should also include notations indicating the amount of product you expect to purchase each month for the next six months and the average price you expect to pay during each of the months. These forecasts not only help to plan for the months ahead, but can also be used after the fact as a measure of the forecasting skills of the people in the purchasing department. Obviously, since commodity prices fluctuate on a relatively broad basis, price forecasts will not always be on target. However, it is interesting to look at price forecasts that have been prepared by several individuals for a particular group of commodities over a specific period of time, and to compare the forecasts with the prices actually paid. Certain people seem to develop a "sixth sense" or a "gut feel" and are consistently more accurate in forecasting commodity prices than others.

Although these price forecasts are a very important communication tool for the purchasing department, they can also be a double-edged sword, since they are a written commitment by the purchasing department regarding price expectations for the future. When they are accurate, little is said, since management feels that that is the purchasing department's job. When they turn out to be inaccurate, however, second guessers emerge from the woodwork to analyze and evaluate why the forecast was wrong and to summarize how they would have done it differently if they had been given an opportunity to do so. After 18 years of such discussions, I have learned to recognize that evaluators will always suggest ways to achieve accuracy. Especially since hindsight is always 20-20.

Communications with Field Operations People

Since someone with only one unit has no need to communicate with field operations people, this is an area that concerns the larger chain. The most obvious type of communication between purchasing and field operations involves data about items being purchased for consumption in the field. This can be relayed through copies of purchase orders, regular weekly or monthly purchasing bulletins to the field, or even periodic meetings between purchasing people and the field operations group. Because these communications tend to become routine, there is often a tendency to neglect them. Under no circumstances should you allow this to happen, since the minute neglect sets in, the effectiveness of the purchasing system diminishes.

Of equal importance for communication to the field is information relating to products not currently being purchased by the organization. Since the purchasing department is frequently the primary source of information about new products, this information must not stop with the purchasing office. The buyer should not be the sole determinant of which products will interest the field people and which will not. Therefore, you should be sure to keep up regular communications relating to new products with both field operations and quality control.

The primary purpose of the buying function is to supply products and services to that arm of the business which services the customer and generates the profit. This group is variously known as "restaurant management," "field operations," or simply "operations." I will refer to them as "operations." The responsibility of purchasing to operations is to channel all available price, supply, and new product information to the operations people as promptly and as thoroughly as possible. Price information is important in forecasting the profitability of the operation and in timing menu price changes. Supply data is also of vital importance, since surpluses can provide an opportunity for special features, while shortages can indicate that a particular product should be deemphasized on the menu.

The tremendous number of new products and product improvements which have been developed over the past decade make this information vital for operations to know. Improved technology in deep fat fryers over the past ten years, for example, has not only revolutionized deep frying procedures, but has also resulted in a new generation of food items that offer new eating experiences. Operations people are generally far too busy managing their businesses to be able to stay abreast of all these new developments. Hence, they must be able to rely on the purchasing function as their eyes and ears in the new product and product improvement marketplaces.

Communications with Marketing and Sales Promotion People

Although the purchasing department is usually considered to be an insignificant factor in a food service company's marketing and promotional plans, the buyer is frequently the one who initiates the promotion or ad campaign by simply alerting the marketing function to the availability of a particular product at an attractive price. While inflation and cost increases have eliminated "All-You-Can-Eat" nights which were so popular in the late 60's and early 70's, attractive price opportunities still allow operations to carry out effective promotions. The products involved in such promotions can range from prime rib of beef to turkey to breaded fish filets to the ever-popular fried chicken or spaghetti. The purchasing department can make a very important contribution to the operating margins in any food service establishment by simply being alert to price bargains on various products and by alerting the marketing and promotion people of these opportunities as far in advance as possible.

Under no circumstances should a marketing group decide to promote a particular item without first checking with the purchasing department as to its price and availability. There are many sad stories involving promotions of a product just as the price began a 50% increase spiral, or as the government closed the fishing grounds, or as the farmers decided to withhold the item from the marketplace. Unless you keep up good communications with both the marketing and sales promotion people, good promotion opportunities may be missed, or even worse, bad promotions may be initiated.

Communications with the Legal Department

When I first began my purchasing career, one of the wise and battle-scarred purchasing veterans I worked under suggested that every buyer should have a good lawyer. While I was surprised by this advice at the time, my experience over the past eighteen years has thoroughly reinforced the wisdom of this comment.

A good lawyer can serve a buyer in two very important ways. First he can help avoid the pitfalls of a bad contract, and second, he can help a buyer extricate himself from a bad contract if he has already signed one. Communications with an attorney or with the legal department should involve keeping the attorney posted on the types of purchase orders being written and on long-term contracts being established. Every time a new type of agreement is received by the purchasing department, it should be sent to an attorney for review. Similarly, the attorney should be informed of any situation where there is any nonperformance on the part of either the vendor or the buyer.

The involvement of an attorney at an early stage will frequently minimize or even entirely avoid unpleasant legal ramifications which can arise from misunderstandings between a buyer and seller. Some people seem to think that buyers and sellers never get into disputes, since the seller will always give in to the buyer in order to get the order or keep the business. This, however, is not always the case. Bitter disputes and acrimonious law suits do break out between buyers and sellers from time to time, and when they do, lawyers are essential.

Communications with Quality Control

There are several different quality considerations that must be considered by the purchasing department and relayed to the quality control area. These involve both monitoring the quality of the product and verifying that suppliers are delivering what has been ordered. Obviously, the product must not be spoiled or in any way unfit for consumption. However, food often comes in that falls short of the specifications given to the vendor. This may include shortcomings in freshness, weight, trim, or cut that cause the operation financial loss.

Let's take a case of lettuce as an example. The lettuce may well be wholesome. Unfortunately, however, six to ten outer leaves per head have browned. These outer leaves must be discarded before the head can be utilized, which means that the restaurant suffers a loss in yield, which in turn increases the cost of its food. In order to correct this situation, the quality control area must communicate on a daily basis with the individual doing the buying. If quality control does not take the initiative in establishing this communication, then the buyer should seek him out and solicit his opinion.

Ordering and delivering fresh meat is also a frequent problem that deserves particular attention. When a buyer specifies a particular cut to the vendor, the vendor should be aware of precisely how much fat (trim) will be permitted as part of the specification. Unless someone in receiving is qualified to evaluate the piece of meat from a fat (trim) standpoint, there may very well be more waste on the product than anticipated. If the receiving person does not compare the amount of wastage on the product with the amount that is permitted under the specifications, the restaurant may lose out.

Incidences of short or overweight on deliveries must also be carefully monitored and communicated. Although overweights are rare, short weights are a recurring malady, especially in those operations with sloppy incoming weighing procedures. If short weight deliveries are permitted, they will quickly become a regular part of the vendor's delivery process.

Thus, the buying office and the individuals responsible for quality control must be in constant contact, with some regular daily procedure whereby they review each other and note any shortcomings. While the urgencies of business can get in the way of such daily reviews, it is the buyer's responsibility to insure that such reviews occur regardless and in spite of other problems.

Communications with Manufacturing People

In establishments that are large enough to have their own commissary or manufacturing facilities, the buyer's communications with the managers of those facilities is an absolute prerequisite to effective purchasing performance. This should consist of far more than the interchange of requisitions, purchase orders, and receiving reports. It should also include regular planning and review sessions to help maximize the flow of information between these two departments. The processing area (any food service commissary or manufacturing operation) must indicate its material requirements to the buying office, giving adequate lead times on any product that is ordered for the first time. They should also distinguish between materials needed for test activities and materials needed for regular processing.

The buying department should forward to the processing area all information about new products and their possible application. It should also contact vendor personnel to help the processing area solve any problem with either the machines or the materials used in connection with them.

Communications with Licensee Operators

With the growth of the major national chains that build their unit base through franchises, the need for the adequate transfer of information to and from licensee operators has grown. Since licensee operators are generally not required to purchase their own equipment, food, or supplies from the franchisor, they have many of the same procurement problems as the individual food service operator. To overcome these obstacles, they therefore usually either join a cooperative buying group established by their fellow licensees or take advantage of special procurement programs set up for their benefit by the franchisor. While they are certainly not forced to participate in these national procurement programs, buying under the umbrella of the franchisor's own volume requirements gives them substantial additional leverage.

Clearly, then, these licensee operators who participate in procurement programs require various kinds of information from the purchasing department. The most effective way of communicating in this situation is to contact the officers of the licensee council or operations group. Trying to communicate on an individual basis with each and every licensed operator is both time-consuming and impractical. However, if an individual licensee has a question or a problem, he should be able to talk on a one-to-one basis with someone in the purchasing department. Thus, the individual operator can obtain the advice and counsel of professional purchasing people when required, while purchasing need not devote a great deal of time and expense to communicating with each and every individual licensee.

The types of information which should emanate from the purchasing department include: new procurement programs that have been set up; forecasts of price and supply conditions for various items; responses to individual procurement problems and offers of professional procurement assistance at any time.

Chapter 17 Questions

1. In outline form, list the various communications contacts and departments which should be maintained by the purchasing department.

2. Describe the type of information which should be communicated from the purchasing department to the financial area of a food service corporation.

3. How can communications between purchasing and the marketing group influence the profitability of a food service operation?

4. Why is communications such an important responsibility of the purchasing department in a food service company?

5. Discuss the steps you would take to insure that the communications program you have outlined in Question #1 is actually being implemented.

18

Centralized Versus Decentralized Purchasing

CONSIDERATIONS REGARDING EACH

No book on purchasing would be complete without a comparison of the pros and cons of centralized versus decentralized purchasing. Although these considerations may be considered academic by the single unit owner, they can give rise to other business considerations which will arise should he expand his operations. Everyone in the food service industry, especially those executives responsible for purchasing activity, should have some idea of which method of procurement is best for his organization. Let's start by listing the benefits and drawbacks of each system.

ADVANTAGES OF CENTRALIZED PROCUREMENT

- Concentration of purchasing volume
- Maximum negotiating leverage
- Standardization of purchasing policy and procedure
- Standardization of products purchased
- Development of highly skilled purchasing personnel
- Concentration of maximum purchasing talent on each procurement situation
- Significant savings in the amount of time spent on procurement
- Ability to develop a broader supplier base

DISADVANTAGES OF CENTRALIZED PROCUREMENT

- Possible time lag between the need and the delivery of the product
- Service problems because the local servicing agency was not a party to the centralized procurement action
- Local distributors who fail to cooperate in programs negotiated by their principal with the central buying office
- Communications problems in getting the word of details of centralized contracts to vendor personnel and company personnel at the local level
- The belief of local operations people that a given central purchase is unattractive because they look at it through the perspective of their own individual operation

ADVANTAGES OF DECENTRALIZED PROCUREMENT

- A greater sense of immediacy in converting the purchase need into the product delivery
- The opportunity to develop a personal relationship between the user/buyer and the vendor
- Improved service performance, since the buyer and the user are usually the same person
- The possibility of lower costs due to the reduction or elimination of freight charges on merchandise that would otherwise be shipped from another area
- The involvement of local operations people in each purchase transaction (In many companies this is considered a drawback)

DISADVANTAGES OF DECENTRALIZED PROCUREMENT

- Benefits that would normally accrue from volume buying dissipated by the substantially lower volume generated on an individual unit basis
- The substantial risk of inconsistency, not only in the quality of the products purchased, but also in the purchasing procedures used

- Time invested in procurement by local operations people interviewing salesmen, requesting quotations, placing orders, examining new products, etc., that could be better spent in an operations capacity

This summary of the pros and cons of both purchasing philosophies can undoubtedly be expanded. However, it does cover the key points of consideration which can help you decide which purchasing method is most effective for your operation.

CONSOLIDATE PURCHASE REQUIREMENTS

The more units that can be lumped together for procurement purposes, the better the procurement job will be. In fact, I myself would attempt to consolidate purchasing requirements as soon as I had more than one unit for which to purchase. I would even carry the theory one step further: If I had only one unit, I would attempt to establish an informal cooperative buying agreement with other single unit operators in my geographical area. By so doing, I would be able to build the volume requirements which the prospective vendors would be invited to bid upon.

It stands to reason that a coffee supplier will be more interested in an account that consumes 100 pounds a week than in an account that consumes 50 pounds per week. Frequently, one owner/manager who is interested in forming a cooperative buying effort will telephone several prospective coffee suppliers informing them of a regular weekly purchase from the co-op and asking them to submit their best selling price offer. This is all the vendors need to recognize the additional business volume available to them under these conditions and consequently "sharpen their pencils" in an effort to submit the most attractive price quotation. This is really the essence of centralized procurement. The more the buyer can maximize his volume, the more he improves his purchasing leverage and, hence, the prices he is able to obtain.

GROUPING ON A REGIONAL BASIS

Although the major food service chains have tended to utilize the centralized procurement method for the last decade or so, certain product groups such as fresh baked goods, dairy products, fresh produce, and certain services such as cleaning, window washing, and pest control simply do not lend themselves to centralization on a corporate-wide basis. However, even in these areas, there is a remarkable opportunity for improving purchasing leverage by grouping the needs of the units on a regional basis, and then constructing purchase arrangements with a number of vendors on an area-by-area basis. While it might be desirable for a 100-unit chain scattered across fifteen states to buy all of its fresh produce from one vendor, handling perishable merchandise over a broad geographic area make this impossible. However, the chain might group its operations on a geographic basis and end up with five locations in one area buying from vendor A, seven locations in another area buying from vendor B, and eleven locations in a third area buying from vendor C. Although purchasing leverage would not be as great as if all 100 units were buying from one vendor, it is still substantially improved. The management of the food service organization should be always alert to the opportunity of consolidating purchase requirements in an effort to maximize price, quality, and service.

EMPLOYEE REACTION

When considering which purchasing philosophy is best for you, it is important to consider how company employees react to each. In the food service industry perhaps more than in other industries, employees seem to have a deep yearning to execute buying responsibility. Centralized purchasing means that such responsibility will be handled by trained and experienced procurement personnel who are specialists in this highly specialized business technique.

With decentralized buying, however, there is always the risk that well-meaning but inexperienced operations personnel will attempt to execute the buying responsibility in a fashion that seems best to them, but which may not be in the best interests of the company. A local manager, for example, may decide that he will be satisfied with 25% fat hamburgers, even though the company's standard specifies a maximum fat content of 18%. By applying his own standard in buying the hamburger, he is not only departing from established company regulations, but also defrauding the public if the company's advertising has stressed the lower fat content of the hamburger. This type of situation develops with amazing regularity when the buying responsibility is decentralized to the local level.

When considering a decentralized program, management should also consider very carefully the ability of their people to properly implement it before making any move in that direction. In my experience, I have found that a well-executed decentralized procurement program requires capabilities and strengths that most food service personnel taken as a whole simply do not have.

While most cases favor centralized purchasing programs, some may still opt for a decentralized system. Hopefully, this chapter has presented the best and worst cases for each so that you can form your own judgment about the appropriate course of action for your particular business.

Chapter 18 Questions

1. Discuss the advantages and disadvantages of centralized procurement.

2. Discuss the advantages and disadvantages of decentralized procurement.

3. Describe how you might set up a regional purchasing program for a multi-unit chain.

4. How does centralized procurement contribute to the development of consistency in the products being purchased?

5. Assume you are the Vice President of Purchasing for a 200-unit chain. Describe and explain the type of procurement program (centralized versus decentralized) that you would install in your operation.

19

The Sales Side of the Buyer's Life

DISPOSING OF USED MATERIALS

Most of the articles we read about purchasing for the food service industry concentrate on innovative approaches to procuring different types of food products. Rarely is there anything in print on the other side of the buyer's life—the sale of surplus or obsolete products. This can contribute important revenues to the company and should therefore not be overlooked as one of the buyer's responsibilities. Even the most mundane products such as garbage and used frying fat can generate revenue for the operation if their disposal is handled in a resourceful manner.

For example, a buyer may find in checking outlying areas near his restaurant that farmers are willing to pick up certain types of garbage at no charge, or even for a nominal payment to the food service establishment. The restaurant's unusable produce and stale bread are very much in demand for certain types of domestic animal feeding programs. Similarly, beef and poultry garbage is often sought by mink farms. How much better it is for the food service operation if the buyer can arrange to have garbage hauled away either at no charge or for a nominal payment by the person removing it, than to have to pay a refuse company a fixed weekly sum.

Similarly, from time to time almost every food service establishment finds itself with an obsolete or unneeded piece of equipment. In most cases this equipment has been fully depreciated during its useful life, so any revenue that can be generated by its sale is "found" money. Unfortunately, many organizations feel that if a piece of equipment is fully depreciated, it is not worth trying to sell and should simply be disposed of.

In fact, nothing could be further from the truth. A very active used equipment marketplace exists in most major metropolitan areas of the United States. Since a dealer in used food service equipment buys low and then sells for a reasonably moderate price, the food service buyer should try to use similar techniques in first consulting with other food service companies to see if they need that particular piece of equipment before he turns to the used equipment buyer. Usually he will get a better price from other companies than he can from the dealer. However, even if such a sale cannot be arranged with another company, it can be sold to the used equipment dealer for a fee. This is certainly preferable to disposing of it via the junk man.

Two other ways to dispose of used equipment are 1) moving equipment, and 2) preparing and circulating a list of available equipment through either the local buyer's association or the local restaurant association in the area. When you move equipment from one unit to another, you get the added benefit of continuing to use a piece of equipment whose history and service record is well known.

If, for example, a gas deep fryer becomes obsolete in a location that has changed to an all-electric kitchen, and if the fryer has been unusually reliable in terms of performance and low maintenance requirements, it is certainly to the firm's advantage to relocate the fryer to another unit that can use it. Often a piece of equipment that shows on the firm's books as having no value can provide three to five years of additional service. This eliminates a one to two thousand dollar expense for a replacement during that period of time. Both common sense and a knowledge of used equipment values and performance are usually the best guidelines in making decisions in this area.

The other disposal alternative simply involves publication of a regular (usually monthly) listing of surplus or soon-to-be surplus equipment. This listing should then be circulated directly to other restaurant operators in the area (as hopefully they would circulate their list to you), or through the local restaurant association. Since it is always preferable to purchase used equipment from some-

SURPLUS EQUIPMENT LIST

ITEM	DESCRIPTION	COST WHEN NEW	AGE	CONDITION	PRICE
Slicer	U.S. Berkel Model #808 semi-automatic slicer—gravity feed with stainless steel blade, easy disassembly for cleaning, long pusher handle for safety, 120 volt 1 phase. Measures 24¼" wide x 26¼" long.	$ 671.50	4 years	Good	$200.00
Convection Oven	G.S. Blodgett Model #EF-112 double stack convection oven, stainless steel front with painted ends and expanded metal back, 208 volt 3 phase.	$2,083.20	4 years	Average	$400.00
Coffee Urn	Blickman Model #CR-44E electric coffee urn—twin 3 gallon with Tomlinson faucets. Brews 27 gallons of coffee per hour, 208 volt 3 phase.	$ 904.00	2½ years	Like New	$550.00
S/S Work Table	Washington Equipment Model #WWT-6-SU S/S urn stand to measure 48" long x 30" deep x 34" high with S/S drain trough, undershelf and back splash.	$ 334.50	6 years	Good	$100.00
Microwave Oven	Litton Model #70/40 microwave oven, 120 volt 1 phase with automatic defroster, six time settings (pushbutton), S/S interior, see-through door.	$ 903.50	2 years	Excellent	$480.00
Rotary Toaster	Savory Model #C-20 rotary toaster with S/S exterior, 208 volt 1 phase. Toasts 800 slices of bread per hour. Can also toast English muffins or hamburger rolls.	$ 334.50	3 years	Average	$100.00

Figure 22

one you know, a listing of this type generally eases the buyer's mind, and benefits both the seller, who wishes to realize something from the disposal, and the buyer, who wants the equipment at the least cost. A sample of the type of used equipment listing that might be prepared by the buyer or local association is shown in Figure 22.

DEVELOP COMPETITIVE BIDS

Although we have not specifically referred to the development of competitive bids on by-product waste and equipment disposal, your approach should involve precisely that. The buyer (who in this case is acting as a seller) should contact at least three firms to obtain the best price, just as he would were he contemplating the purchase of an item. When he is negotiating a purchase, the buyer will usually find a fairly well-defined market price structure among the vendors he contacts. On the sales side, buyers are frequently amazed to find a wide disparity between the prices that prospective purchasers are willing to pay. In view of this disparity, it is obviously best when disposing of the equipment to get as many different purchase offerings as possible.

WARRANTIES

During the course of negotiating the sale of surplus or obsolete equipment, the buyer will frequently be asked if he will guarantee or warrantee the performance of the item. This can be a very risky business and should be avoided in most cases. It stands to reason that the older a piece of equipment, the greater the potential for breakdown or erratic performance. This is the reason that an appliance repair service charges a progressively higher fee for its annual service contract as an appliance gets older.

The person attempting to dispose of a used piece of equipment should always remember that his objective is disposal—clear and complete—with no strings attached. Any type of performance guarantee given to the buyer can obstruct this objective. If the prospective buyer insists on receiving such a guarantee, the seller would be well advised to remind him that the low sales price in part reflects the absence of the guarantee, and that if the guarantee is all that important, perhaps a new piece of equipment should be purchased instead.

CHARITABLE DONATIONS

Another approach to disposal which is normally used only as a last resort is the donation of an item to a recognized charitable institution. When such a donation is made, the donating organization receives credit for the current value of the item and can take a deduction in this amount on its income tax return.

An additional benefit to be derived from the donation of surplus food or equipment is the very positive public relations impact both with members of the organization to whom the donation is made and also with the general public if there is appropriate media coverage. Many of the nation's most successful restaurateurs have enhanced their image through public relations efforts like these.

In summary, by-product and scrap disposal is an important responsibility that should rest with the buyer for the food service organization. It should always be considered as a source of additional revenue, and should therefore receive as much attention as would a buying decision.

Chapter 19 Questions

1. Why is the sale of obsolete equipment and surplus materials an important consideration in the buyer's job?

2. As a buyer for a food service company, you are asked to dispose of two obsolete pieces of equipment that are in perfectly good working condition: a gas operated deep fryer and a microwave oven. List the steps you would take to arrange for the disposal of these items.

3. How can a buyer best keep up with potential sales outlets for obsolete equipment and materials?

4. What type of representations/warranties should a buyer be prepared to make in conjunction with the sale of obsolete equipment?

5. How can the buyer best insure that his firm is receiving maximum value for its obsolete and surplus materials?

20

Services Available to the Food Service Industry

SERVICES ARE PURCHASES TOO

When discussing the range of products that a typical food service buyer purchases, we usually focus our attention on food items. Secondary emphasis is given to the paper goods, cleaning supplies, and equipment that are necessary for the preparation and service of the food. But rarely do we consider how to purchase the services which are so important to the orderly operation of the business.

Included in the "services" category would be such requirements as cleaning services, maintenance contracts on equipment no longer under warranty, pest control services, garbage and refuse removal, landscaping services, laundry, and utility consultants. Perhaps the reason we hear so little about these services is that many food service operations consider them not as purchases, but rather as necessary annoyances that occur during the normal course of the business. This attitude is unfortunate, since expenditures for these services represent a net cash drain which comes right off the bottom line of the profit and loss statement. Hence, anything that can be done to decrease the expense of these services while maintaining their quality increases the profitability of the food service operation.

A contract for laundry services or landscaping care should be negotiated with a minimum of three potential suppliers, just as the purchase of baked goods, produce, or seafood would be. Usually service contracts are negotiated on an annual basis in order to provide the buyer with the maximum amount of purchasing leverage as he enters into the negotiation. Since the purchase consideration in arranging for each of these services varies widely, let us consider each of them individually.

CLEANING SERVICES

Although many food service operations do their own cleaning, certain kinds of cleaning services must be purchased on the outside. Rug shampooing, floor stripping and polishing, and window and drapery cleaning, for example, are normally handled by professional cleaning organizations. In arranging for such services, the buyer should prepare a specification list outlining precisely what services he seeks, with as much detail as possible regarding the manner and frequency with which they are to be performed. This specification should also include the security provisions such as bonding and prior security checks on cleaning personnel (since they are frequently on the premises after hours) which the buyer wishes to impose. If a key is to be given to an employee of the cleaning company, there should be agreement as to how to handle it if employee turnover occurs. By first preparing a written summary of all of these requirements and then forwarding it to a minimum of three cleaning contractors for the preparation of competitive bids, the buyer will assure himself of getting the most attractive proposal available.

GARBAGE AND REFUSE DISPOSAL

Although contracting for these services in a major metropolitan area can frequently be very frustrating, the buyer should still attempt to compare at least three private cartage companies before entering into a disposal agreement. In addition to the rate charged for the removal of garbage and refuse, the buyer should also consider the frequency of pickup, the type of containers that will be used (plastic bags, heavy duty plastic barrels, and stationary iron refuse bins), and the contractor's responsibility for cleaning up any garbage spilled after each pickup.

Agreements regarding all of these elements should be hammered out before the contract is awarded, since afterwards it will be too late to get additional commitments. In those areas where obtaining a number of competitive bids is difficult, the buyer can frequently obtain concessions in the form of these other elements while dealing with only one company. Remember that although ten or twenty or fifty dollars per week for garbage and refuse removal may not seem like a lot of money, it can add up to a substantial sum by the end of a year.

PEST CONTROL SERVICES

Although no one likes to admit it, many food service operations must use periodic pest control procedures to eliminate or prevent insect and rodent problems. Pest control requirements vary widely, depending upon the geographic location of the establishment and the climatic conditions at any given time of year. The pest control industry has grown rapidly in recent years, with a number of nationally franchised firms competing with independent businessmen in the local area. However, a quick walk through the yellow pages should provide more than enough potential contacts to set the stage for competitive proposals from at least three firms.

As with any service, the buyer should prepare a detailed written statement of requirements so that all bidders will prepare their quotations on the same premise. It is also an excellent idea to ask for and check references from a potential firm. Occasionally a prospective vendor will present references who, when checked, will inform you that the vendor either had not done any work for the firm or has not completed the job satisfactorily. The few minutes that it takes to check these references can save the buyer hours of aggravation and duplicated effort for work poorly done.

In seeking the competitive bids on pest control services, the buyer should propose a fixed period of time (at least a year) and a set list of procedures to be completed on a periodic basis (either every two weeks or once a month) at a fixed monthly fee. In addition, the agreement should provide for emergency or special services on an as-needed basis with the fee to be computed on either a time-and-materials basis or on a flat-rate charge per visit. If you check with local agents of the national pest control companies, you can frequently arrange a multi-unit contract that provides lower per unit rates than those available from local vendors.

LANDSCAPING SERVICES

The best time for the food service buyer to make arrangements for landscaping services is in the middle of winter. At that time landscape companies are usually at their lowest work level and are lining up new business for the spring and summer months. The written statement of requirements, competitive proposals, and reference checks should of course precede any commitments. Since landscape contractors frequently engage in snow removal as a means of supplementing their income during the lean winter months, you may want to include snow removal in the overall landscaping contract. This may help you obtain price concessions on snow removal from a firm that is anxious to get the landscaping business.

LAUNDRY SERVICES

Laundry services are a more complex purchase consideration, since besides all the pre-contract requirements, the buyer is also faced with whether to purchase laundry services on the outside or to install his own laundry equipment on the premises. As laundry charges have escalated, and as no-iron fabrics have become more popular, the costs of in-house laundry systems are often considerably less than the charges for outside laundry services.

In determining this question for himself, the buyer should accumulate his laundry expenses for a one-year period, including any fees that are charged for product replacements, and compare them against the cost of a laundry system (washer and dryer) and the supplies and manpower necessary to operate them. By spreading the capital cost of the equipment itself over the estimated useful life (usually three to five years), and then adding in the cost of labor and supplies, the buyer is able to determine quite accurately the cost of an in-house laundry system. He can then compare this figure with the annual cost of outside laundry services to see which is more practicable.

Although this opportunity may not be feasible in very small food service operations, the buyer can save money by asking his detergent supplier to help him obtain quotations for the laundry equipment. Since the detergent supplier deals with laundry firms and equipment regularly, he should have special insights in this area that can be very helpful. He should also get several quotations on his own. By comparing the supplier's quotation with those developed independently, the buyer can be assured of getting the best price possible.

In the event that the analysis favors outside laundry service, the buyer should spell out precisely how the responsibility for lost or damaged merchandise will be handled. This is necessary because 1) the ever-present problem of employee pilferage occurs not only in food service establishments but also in other businesses such as laundry companies, and 2) the automatic, high speed equipment now in use in most commercial laundry operations sometimes damages the merchandise either through mangling or through excessive wear and tear. If the laundry is to be responsible for the replacement of lost or damaged merchandise, the buyer should get this commitment in writing and attempt to evaluate what price premium he is being charged for this protection. If the laundry will not take responsibility for lost or damaged merchandise, then the buyer should attempt to develop some historical information on the number of pieces that will need to be replaced each year and thet total cost of such replacement. Any buyer entering into a laundry agreement without this information firmly in hand is running the risk of finding very unpleasant surprises.

UTILITY CONSULTANTS

Although utility consultants have been in business for many years, the recent energy crisis in the United States has made them a far more visable factor in the industrial marketplace. These people earn their living by evaluating a firm's utility expenditures (including telephone, water, gas, electricity, steam, and oil consumption) in order to find areas where the firm can reduce its usage rates. Utility consultants normally operate on a contingency fee basis, collecting 50% of any savings actually realized. Because of the tremendous impact of higher energy costs on the profit and loss statement, utility consultants can be of significant value to the buyer.

However, there is a caveat which the buyer should be fully aware of before entering into any agreement with such organizations. These firms generally require the "client" to agree to share the savings for a five-year period from the date of implementation. However, achieving the savings that have been identified often requires substantial capital investments. But if the food service organization chooses not to make those capital expenditures due to an unfavorable return on investment required, the utility consultant may still attempt to claim a fee for identifying the potential savings. In order to avoid unpleasant legal entanglements, it is essential that the buyer have a full written proposal from the utility consultant before entering into any agreement with him. Specific attention should be paid to the handling of fees on recommendations made by the consultant but not implemented by the food service company.

VENDING SERVICES

Although some food service establishments own their own vending machines, the vast majority of machines are the property of outside vending companies. Vending machines in a food service establishment should be looked upon as a significant additional source of revenue for the operator. Unfortunately, a great many of the vending machines placed in such establishments do not yield anywhere near the return to the establishment that they should. This results from a combination of factors including machine inefficiency, commission payments from the vending company that are below competitive rates, deliberate or inadvertant short counts on the number of units of merchandise sold in each period, and inferior merchandise that fails to attract maximum consumer interest.

In making arrangements for vending services, the buyer should make certain that he receives new, up-to-date, modern and well-maintained equipment, that his commission payments are competitive with those offered by other vending firms in the area, that every machine has an electronic meter installed on the interior to record the number of vends registered on that machine, and that nothing but top quality merchandise is used in the machines. If these four factors are under control, the chances of maximizing the return from the vending machines will be greatly enhanced.

Chapter 20 Questions

1. Describe the steps the buyer should take in soliciting quotations on service contracts.

2. What additional factors should be included in the development of quotations for cleaning services?

3. How should the buyer determine whether to use an outside laundry service or an in-house laundry system?

4. Describe the role of the utility consultant in providing services to the food service industry.

5. What are the major problem areas that can crop up with an outside vending contractor, and how should they be corrected?

21

The Concept of Materials Management

MATERIALS MANAGEMENT DEFINED

During the 1970's a new business technique called *materials management* gained increasing popularity in all segments of business involving a manufacturing or processing operation. Basically, it says that all functions relating to the flow of raw materials into, and finished goods out of, an operation should be tied together. This means that all activities essential in procuring raw and packaging materials, transporting these materials to the point of manufacture, inspecting and accepting incoming materials, storing these materials until the time of actual use, returning the materials to storage after they are manufactured into a finished product, storing them until they are shipped to the point of ultimate use, processing such a shipment, and advance planning of these functions: All should be lumped together under the heading of "materials management." Since all of these activities are interrelated, they should be looked on as "parts of the whole" rather than as individual and independent activities.

The philosophy of materials management grew from a number of management consulting studies done on various types of businesses during the 1960's. Rather than having these various functions operate independently of one another, the materials management approach coordinates, integrates, and consolidates these various activities into one smooth, harmonious flow.

All of the activities included in materials management can be looked upon as the support services necessary to execute an effective and economical manufacturing or assembling operation. The only area specifically excluded from the materials management concept is the actual manufacturing or processing activity, or, in the case of the food service industry, the actual preparation of the food in the kitchen.

As the use of this concept has expanded during the past five years, its applications to fields not normally associated with direct manufacturing activities has increased. The food service industry is an excellent example, and I believe that a fitting way to conclude this text on purchasing for the food service industry is to examine ways in which the broad concept of materials management applies to our industry. The concept and philosophy of materials management provide an effective umbrella under which we can pull the various individual areas of purchasing together to produce an effective procurement system for a food service company. Although most of the specific activities normally included in the materials management function are not direct responsibilities of a purchasing department, the buying personnel have enough daily contact with these other functions to require that they be totally familiar with them.

In order to simplify the example of how materials management can be applied in the food service industry, let us take the most fundamental unit of the industry—the individually owned and operated restaurant—as a starting point. After first looking at materials management in this framework, you can then make extensions and applications to larger, more complex food service operations.

In the individual unit operation, the owner/manager runs a business which essentially prepares and serves food to a group of customers. In order to accomplish this goal the owner/manager must first have the necessary facilities to prepare and serve the food, sufficient financial resources to support these facilities, sufficient materials and labor to perform the function, and the know-how to supervise the operation. To the uninitiated, that may sound like a fairly complete summary of the essential elements of running a food service establishment.

However, those of us in the business might respond by saying, "If only those were the only things we had to worry about!" Because in addition to these basic requirements, the owner/manager must also be concerned about where the needed materials necessary will come from, how much he will pay for them, how they will get to his location, where he will store them until they are ready for use, where he will store them after they have been processed but before they have been delivered to the customer, and how they will be delivered to the customer. These considerations form the nucleus of the concept of materials management as it is applied to the food service industry. Each of these functions is important to the successful execution of the overall food service operation. How well they can be pulled together and coordinated will have a direct bearing on the efficiency of the overall operation.

TWO EXAMPLES OF POOR MANAGEMENT COORDINATION

Since the owner/manager of the single unit food service operation may be performing these functions himself, he will try to achieve maximum coordination as he executes them. Surprisingly, however, even in situations where one person performs all these functions, this coordination is often lacking. For example, a vendor may be asked to make a delivery without specific directions as to the time of delivery required. Through no fault of his own, the vendor's truck driver arrives at the restaurant at 12:30 PM—the peak of the lunch period. Since the owner/manager is busy either working the grill, collecting cash, supervising the overall operation, or doing all three, he is in no position to check in the shipment being delivered. Consequently, he may keep the truck driver waiting for more than an hour. If the driver becomes annoyed, he may fail to notify the owner/manager of some broken packages which are not discovered until two days later, when they have leaked all over the storeroom.

While I won't bore you with the rest of this actual story, which insured total dissatisfaction between the supplier and the buyer, suffice it to say that all this aggravation and agony could have been avoided. Had there been coordination between the purchase of the material and the timing of its delivery, the arrival of the merchandise would not have conflicted with more important activities going on in the food service establishment at the actual delivery time. Although this is rather a basic example of how a materials management approach can benefit the food service industry, it is far from an isolated example and happens just as often in the larger food service establishments.

Similarly, the lack of coordination between the purchasing office and the people responsible for maintaining finished goods inventory records caused one operation substantial inventory obsolescense. This happened when one fast food chain decided to expand their menu and increase their average check by promoting three different flavored pies in their units. Because they were unable to find exactly what they wanted in the commercial marketplace, however, they approached a large regional bakery and asked them to manufacture a product to their specifications.

All went well for approximately six months, as the purchasing department ordered the pies for direct shipment to an outside warehouse which handled the firm's distribution requirements. However, after six months of aggressive advertising and promotional support of the individual pies in their units, the senior management decided that they were not getting a sufficient return on the marketing funds expended on the pie promotion. Therefore, they decided to replace it with another item.

Although this decision had been widely discussed within the organization, it somehow failed to reach the individual responsible for inventory replenishment. That person ordered several truckloads of the item a few days after the effective date of the discontinuance. Before the oversight was noticed, the vendor had produced the pies and shipped them to the outside warehouse. The outside warehouse, not having been notified to the contrary, accepted the pies and put them in inventory. It was only at month's end, two weeks later, when the outside warehouse sent in its inventory report that management became aware of the problem that they had obsolete individual pies.

Since the item had been manufactured expressly for that company, there was a very limited potential for resale to some other food service operator. The sad result was that the company ended up selling the pies for 30¢ on the dollar (30% of their original cost) to a liquidator who shipped them out of the country. The entire fiasco could have been avoided had the fundamental concepts of materials management been in force at the time.

The food service industry is replete with examples of poor coordination that results in operating inefficiencies and actual dollar losses. The operator of the large or the small food service establishment can best avoid this type of difficulty by looking at the entire flow of materials through his operation from the time he sees the need for some material until it has been delivered to the final consumer. Each step in this process is interrelated and interconnected. By developing a natural flow from one step to another, the operator will not only avoid the pitfalls of poor coordination, but will also create a smoother, more efficient, and usually more rapid processing of materials through his unit.

APPLICATION TO FOOD SERVICE

Lest anyone conclude that materials management is only for the manufacturing segment of the food service industry, let me take the analogy one step further. The individually owned and operated coffee shop which caters primarily to an on-the-run breakfast and luncheon type customer can employ the principals of materials management with equal impact on their operation as would a massive steel mill or auto assembly plant.

Very simply, the coordination of ordering, receiving, and storing incoming raw and packaging materials so that they are always available to the kitchen personnel (the manufacturing process), and the establishment of a smooth system for the orderly delivery of orders from the kitchen to the customer, whether for consumption on the premises or off, as in a take-out business, all require the fundamental principals of materials management

Ironically, the very simplicity of the process tends to mislead people into feeling that it is either unimportant or ineffective in the food service operation. However, as the food service company increases in size, and particularly if it develops its own manufacturing (commissary operations), or distribution facility, the importance of materials management principles increases dramatically.

VERTICAL INTEGRATION

Over the past century as industrial companies have grown in size, there has been a definite tendency toward vertical integration of their manufacturing operations. Vertical integration means self-manufacture of component parts needed to make the finished product. A prime example of this trend can be seen in the automobile industry, where the larger the company grew, the more it became involved in the manufacture of self-assembly parts. Hence, today we see auto companies owning factories that produce spark plugs, window glass, radios, and even the steel that is used to fabricate the automobiles. This correlation between size and vertical integration has not been lost on the food service industry. Its most prominent example can be found in the numerous food service companies that have chosen to establish their own central commissary rather than to produce duplicate products at each individual food service outlet.

The initial food service commissaries developed in New York City during the early 1920's, when both the Schrafft's and Horn & Hardart organizations had central commissaries that prepared a substantial portion of the food served in their restaurants and then delivered it fresh daily throughout their chain. Although very primitive operation in the 1920's, this basic concept can now be seen in the multimillion dollar manufacturing and distribution facilities operated by such food service giants as Howard Johnson's, Marriott, and Burger King. These companies, and many others, have concluded that their growth has warranted the self-manufacture and self-distribution approach to vertical integration. Obviously, different approaches are designed to fit different food service companies.

Perhaps the single most important factor in the expansion of vertically integrated companies in the food service industry was the rapid growth and consumer acceptance of frozen foods during the 1960's. Prior to the advent of frozen foods as a way of life in the food service industry, a commissary operation was limited to the amount of food it could process and distribute fresh within a twenty-four hour period. However, once frozen foods became the stock in trade of the food service industry, previous limitations on production and distribution capacities were essentially obliterated. The only factors now governing the quantity of food to be processed, and the distance over which it will be distributed, are the locations of the individual units in a chain and the economics of distributing materials to them.

Some food service companies that have as few as three or four units who have found it economical and efficient to prepare their food on a central basis. Obviously, as the size of any food service operation increases, the economics and efficiencies of a commissary increase in proportion to their size.

As we recognize this very real trend in the food service industry, we can see even more clearly why the concept of materials management will continue to expand in our industry. One has only to glance at the employment pages of the Sunday *New York Times* or at various trade magazines to notice the increase in job opportunities that require experience in the area of materials management. Where companies were once content to hire a plant manager or a department foreman, they are now seeking production control analysts, inventory planning supervisors, and raw material controllers. Suffice it to say that since the materials management approach is of growing importance in the food industry, any individual planning on a career in the purchasing area should become familiar with this concept as a part of his basic purchasing training.

Chapter 21 Questions

1. What elements do you feel should be included in a materials management program for a food service company?

2. How do you see a materials management program contributing to the operational efficiency of a food service company?

3. Describe the relationship between the size of a food service organization and the need for materials management programs.

4. In your judgment which elements in the materials management program are most important? Why?

5. How can a buyer for a food service organization best utilize the principles of materials management?

Appendix

SOURCES OF INFORMATION

Since a key ingredient in the successful purchasing function is the buyer's ability to continually keep himself abreast of new market developments, I would like to summarize in this section the sources of information which are available to the buyer and which provide daily, weekly, and monthly updates on the supply and price movements of key commodity items utilized in the food service industry.

THE U.S.D.A.

The primary source of such information comes from the U.S. Department of Agriculture and various state agricultural agencies.

The best starting place for a buyer who wishes to develop additional market information is the U.S. Department of Agriculture, publications unit, in Washington, D.C. 20250. This department publishes a pamphlet listing the numerous commodity and crop reports which are issued by its various offices around the United States. This pamphlet contains a listing of the reports, an indication of the subject matter covered, and details as to frequency of issue, cost, if any, and ordering procedures. Included in the various reports issued by the

U.S. Department of Agriculture are detailed facts on beef and veal, pork products, poultry, vegetables (by area of the country), citrus fruits, seafood, milk, butter, eggs, and cheese.

Another helpful source of information are the periodic reports issued by the Department of Agriculture summarizing government purchases of various commodities for activities such as school lunch programs. I have found that an analysis of prices paid by the government from period to period can provide some interesting insights into the general trend of commodity price movements. It can also indicate the intensity of the efforts made by various suppliers to obtain government contracts. Frequently vendors will solicit government business much more aggressively during slow economic times than they will during periods of greater business prosperity. It never ceases to surprise me how much information of this type is available if the buyer takes the time to search for it. Contact the Agricultural Marketing Service, U.S.D.A., Washington D.C. 20250 for information on obtaining these reports.

THE WALL STREET JOURNAL

Another obvious and very complete source of commodity information is the *Wall Street Journal*. For 25¢ per copy it is probably the most concise and up-to-date source of supply and price information that a food service buyer can obtain. It also gives up-to-date information on such factors as weather conditions, labor contracts, government actions, export sales, etc., that can directly effect the supply and price of various commodity items. A subscription may be ordered from Dow Jones & Co. Inc., 200 Burnett Road, Chicopee, Mass. 01020 ($45 per year).

There are actually three different types of commodity information contained in the *Wall Street Journal* each day. First, there is a summary of futures market trading in domestic commodity markets from the previous business day. As we noted in Figure 10 in Chapter 5, a large number of commodity futures have a direct relationship with items consumed in the food service operation. Second, there is a summary table of cash prices paid by commodity, which includes a reference to the price recorded on the previous business day as well as on the same day one year earlier. A regular scanning of this cash price chart will provide the buyer with an excellent means of developing a feel for the direction of various commodity price movements. Third, there is the daily commodity commentary which provides an in-depth analysis of a different commodity situation each day, as well as a brief summary of key developments in each of the major commodity markets on the previous trading day. A daily review of this type of information should put the average buyer for the food service operation in an excellent position to know his markets.

Various trade journals such as *Nations Restaurant News, Hospitality, Restaurant Business, Cooking for Profit,* and *Drive-In Food Service* also contain information on product, price, and supply. While this information can be of benefit to the buyer, he should realize that due to publication schedules, the information in these periodicals is not nearly as timely as that contained in the daily press.

For the buyer really interested in developing an in-depth market knowledge, there are additional publications issued in newsletter form by The American Institute for Food Distribution, Inc., 28-06 Broadway, Fairlawn, N.J. 07410, and The Kipplinger Washington Editors, 1729 H St., N.W., Washington, D.C. 20006. A note to any of the above will bring full ordering details and price information.

Commodity letters can be obtained, usually gratis, from brokerage firms such as Merrill Lynch, Pierce, Fenner and Smith, Bache and Co., Inc., and E. F. Hutton, and Co.

Index

Accounting department, 152
Agriculture, U.S. Department of (U.S.D.A.), 229–30
Alcoholic beverages, 108–17
Approval for purchases, 15
Authority, buying, 15–16
Availability
   of food items, menu planning and, 91–92
   of frozen prepared (portion control) foods, 104

Bidding, competitive, 26–29
   in capital equipment purchases, 139–40
   on waste and equipment disposal, 210
Brands of liquor, 112–14
Budget
   capital-equipment provisions in, 142–43
   purchasing, 193–94

Buyers, *see* Personnel, purchasing
Buying authority, 15–16
Buying hedge, 75–76
Buying plan, 63
   developing a basic, 95–99
Buying strategy, 60–80
   considerations in establishing a, 63–69
      long-term, fixed price method of purchasing, 64–68
   definition of, 60
   examples of, 60, 62–63
   hedging in commodity futures markets and, 69–78
   implementation of, 63
   timing as factor in, 78–79
By-product disposal, 207–11

Call brands, 113
Capital, leasing vs. purchasing decision and availability of, 56

Capital equipment, 137–45
  budget provisions for, 142–43
  definition of, 137
  financial controls and, 141–43
  forecasting requirements for, 141–42
  identification and inventorying of, 143
  installation of, 140
  selection of vendors of, 138–39
  used, 143–44
  warranty and service responsibility for, 140–41
  See also Equipment
Carrying charge arrangement, 39, 42
Cash discounts, 52–53
Centralized purchasing, 5–6, 17–18, 203–5
  advantages and disadvantages of, 201–2
  employee reaction to, 204–5
Chains of restaurants, 6–7
  organization chart for, 11
Chef or cook, inefficiency due to procurement by, 5
Cleaning services, 214
Cleaning supplies, 124–26
Commodity futures markets, 69–78
Communications, 191–99
  with field operations people, 194–95
  with financial people, 193–94
  guidelines to follow for, 191–93
  with legal department, 196–97
  with licensee operators, 198–99
  with manufacturing people, 198
  with marketing and sales promotion people, 195–96
  with quality control department, 197–98
Competitive bidding, 26–29
  in capital equipment purchases, 139–40
  on waste and equipment disposal, 210
Computers, purchase orders prepared by, 150
Contracts, purchase
  long-term, fixed price, 64–68
  price determination in, 42–46
Convection oven, 105
Cooperatives, purchasing, 18–21
Costs, fixed vs. controllable, 3
Count, as quality control tool, 173

Decentralized purchasing
  advantages and disadvantages of, 202–3
  employee reaction to, 204–5
Deliveries
  emergency, 93–94
  by liquor distributors, 116
  number of, per week, 54
  special requirements for, 93–94
  storage capacity and, 93
  time of, 54
  See also Receiving merchandise; Shipments
Delivery arrangements, 53–54
Delivery days, 54
Delivery schedules, 96–97
Demand and supply, *see* Supply and demand

Discount arrangements, 52–53
Dispensing equipment, 128–34
Disposal
  garbage, 214–15
  of waste and used equipment, 211
Distributors
  liquor, selection of, 112, 115–17
  See also Vendors

Efficiency
  purchasing, 185–88
  purchasing activities which can reduce, 4–6
Emergency shipments, terms relating to, 55
Employees, *see* Personnel, purchasing; *and individual types of employees*
Equipment
  capital, *see* Capital equipment
  charitable donations of, 211
  easy-to-operate, 178–79
  used
    buying of, 143–44
    disposing of, 207–11
Equipment programs, 128–34
  advantages of, 132
  guidelines for, 132–34

Field operations people, communications with, 194–95
Fixed price contracts, 42–46
  long-term, 64–68
Food specifications, *see* Specifications
Forecasts
  of capital equipment requirements, 141–42
  of prices, 157–59
  of supply/demand trends, 35
  See also Projections
Freezer space, 92–93
  for portion control items, 105
Frozen foods, shelf life of, 94
Frozen prepared (portion control) foods, 102–6
  advantages of, 103–4
Future needs, projecting, 156–57

Garbage disposal, 207, 214–15
Grouping on a regional basis, 203–4

Hedge, buying, 75–76
Hedging in commodity futures market, 69–78

Iced broiler futures, hedging in, 72–74
Identification of capital equipment, 143
Individual restaurants, organization chart for, 10
Inefficiency, purchasing activities which can increase, 4–6
Insect problems, 215
Inventorying of capital equipment, 143

Job descriptions for purchasing personnel, 9, 13–14

Landscape services, 216
Laundry services, 216–17
Leasing equipment, purchasing vs., 56, 58
Legal department, communications with, 196–97

Licensee operators, communications with, 198–99
Liquor, 108–17
  brands of, 112–14
  postoffs in buying, 110–12, 116
Liquor distributors, selecting, 112, 115–17
Long-term, fixed price method of purchasing, 64–68

Management coordination, 223–25
Manufacturers, communications with, 198
Market conditions, knowing current, 37
Market price
  current, purchasing on the basis of, 68–69
  date-of-shipment method of price determination, 42–46
  quotation sheets, for price determination, 45–46
Marketing department, communications with, 195–96
Materials management, 221–27
  definition of, 221–22
Meat Buyer's Guide to Portion Control Meat Cuts, The (National Association of Meat Purveyors), 95
Meat Buyer's Guide to Standardized Meat Cuts, The (National Association of Meat Purveyors), 95
Meat in the Food Service Industry (National Live Stock and Meat Board), 95

Meat purchasing, buying plan and, 95
Menu, price and availability of items as considerations in planning, 91–92
Microwave ovens, 105
Minimum order quantity, 25
Minimum order requirement, 53

National Association of Meat Purveyors, 95
National Live Stock and Meat Board, 95
New pack time, 37

Obsolescence of equipment, leasing vs. purchasing decision and, 58
One-stop shopping, 97–98
Operating supplies, 124–26
Opportunity buys, 47–52
  definition of, 47
  determining the value of, 47–48
  example of, 48–52
  profit plan protection and, 52
Ordering, inefficiency in, 4
Orders
  minimum, 25, 53
  placing, terms relating to, 55
  purchase, 149–50, 193
Organization charts, 9–11
Organization of purchasing, 9–22
  buying authority and approval and, 15–16
  centralization, *see* Centralized purchasing
  on commodity basis, 17
  cooperative buying organizations and, 18–21

geographical, 17
guidelines for, 9
  job descriptions, 13–14
  organization charts, 10–12
  limitation of number of qualified purchasers and, 16–17
  See also specific topics
Ovens, 105
Overseas purchasing of tabletop items, 121

Packaging, specifications as to, 82–83
Packer's specification, 90
Past purchasing activity, future purchases and, 155–56
Personnel, purchasing
  job descriptions for, 9, 13–14
  qualities important in, 161–63
  training of, 163–66
Pest control services, 215
Physical capabilities of an operation, 92–93
Portion control foods
  advantages of, 103–4
  definition of, 101–2
  equipment considerations for, 105–6
Postoffs, 110–12, 116
Poultry purchasing, buying plan and, 95–96
Pour brands, 113
Precooked meals, *see* Frozen prepared foods
Preparation time and steps, buying plan and, 98–99
Price cycles, annual, 38–41
Price determination in purchase contracts, 42–46

Price forecasts, 157–59
Price reductions (postoffs), 110–12, 116
Price/value relationship (quality), 3, 33
  value analysis and, 184–85
Prices
  fixed, in purchase contracts, 42–46
  long-term, 64–68
  market, *see* Market price
Profits, purchasing and, 2–3
Projections
  of future needs, 156–57
  See also Forecasts
Purchase contracts
  long-term, fixed price, 64–68
  price determination in, 42–46
Purchase order, 149–50, 193
Purchasing
  centralization of, *see* Centralized purchasing
  importance of, 1–2
  organization of, *see* Organization of purchasing
  profits influenced by, 2–3
  See also specific topics
Purchasing budget, 193–94
Purchasing cooperatives, 18–21
Purchasing department, communications of, *see* Communications
  quality control department and, relationship between, 169–74
Purchasing efficiency, 185–88
Purchasing personnel, *see* Personnel, purchasing
Purchasing procedures and controls, 147–52

overview of, 147–48
training of personnel in, 163–66
See also Quality control
Purchasing requisition, 148–49

Quality (price/value relationship), 3, 33
value analysis and, 184–85
Quality control, 152–54, 174
count and, 173
specification of procedures to be used for, 83
Quality control department, 151–52
communications with, 197–98
purchasing function and, relationship between, 169–74

Rebates by liquor distributors, 116–17
Receiving merchandise, detailing procedures to be used in, 83
Receiving report, 151–52
Requisition, purchasing, 148–49
Restaurant failures, 2
Restaurants
chains of, 6–7
organization chart for, 11
individual, organization chart for, 10
small, 6–7
Rodent problems, 215

Sales promotion people, communications with, 195–96
Seafood purchasing, buying plan and, 95–96
Service
leasing vs. purchasing question and availability of, 56, 58
responsibility for, capital equipment purchases and, 140–41
Service programs, 177, 178
Services
cleaning, 214
landscaping, 216
laundry, 216–17
negotiating contracts for, 213–14
pest control, 215
Shelf life, 94
Shipments
emergency, terms relating to, 55
See also Deliveries
Shipping instruction, 150–51
Small restaurants, 6–7
Source selection, 23–32
competitive bidding and, 26–29
definition of, 23
steps in, 23–25
vendor relations and, 29–30
Special services of vendor, source selection and, 30–31
Specifications
examples of, 84–89
giving complete, 81–83
packer's, 90
for quality control, 83
for receiving merchandise, 83
variations in product and, 90–91
Stockless purchasing of tabletop items, 122–23
Storage capacity, 92–93
delivery schedules and, 97

Suppliers, *see* Vendors
Supply and demand, basic laws of, 34–37
Supply contracts, *see* Purchase contracts
Supply/demand cycles, 37
Systematization of purchasing activities, inefficiency due to partial, 4–5

Tabletop items, 119–24
  overseas purchasing of, 121
  stockless purchasing of, 122–23
Timing efficiency, value analysis and, 186–88
Timing of purchases, 38
Trade journals, 231

Urner-Barry Report, 45
Used equipment
  buying, 143–44
  disposing of, 207–11
Utility consultants, 217–18

Value analysis, 183–88
Vending machines, 218
Vendors (suppliers)
  of capital equipment, selecting, 138–39
  come-ons of, 180–81
  quality control/purchasing function relationship and, 172–73
  relations with, 29–30, 179–80
  reliability of, checking on, 177–78
  responsibilities of buyer to, 181–82
  special services provided by, source selection and, 30–31
  terms available from, 52–56
  See also Deliveries; Distributors; Source selection
Vertical integration, 225–26

Wall Street Journal, 230–31
Warranty
  for capital equipment, 140–41
  on used equipment, 210–11
Waste control reports, 154–55
Well brand, 113
Wines, 114–15
Worth of an item, determining, 33–34

Yellow Sheet, 45
Yield analyses, 154
Yields, 184